S. HRG. 114–300

WORLDWIDE THREATS

HEARING

BEFORE THE

COMMITTEE ON ARMED SERVICES
UNITED STATES SENATE

ONE HUNDRED FOURTEENTH CONGRESS

FIRST SESSION

FEBRUARY 26, 2015

Printed for the use of the Committee on Armed Services

Available via the World Wide Web: http://www.fdsys.gov/

U.S. GOVERNMENT PUBLISHING OFFICE

20–720 PDF WASHINGTON : 2016

For sale by the Superintendent of Documents, U.S. Government Publishing Office
Internet: bookstore.gpo.gov Phone: toll free (866) 512–1800; DC area (202) 512–1800
Fax: (202) 512–2104 Mail: Stop IDCC, Washington, DC 20402–0001

(II)

CONTENTS

FEBRUARY 26, 2015

	Page
WORLDWIDE THREATS	1
Clapper, James R., Director of National Intelligence	4
Stewart, Lt. Gen. Vincent, Director of the Defense Intelligence Agency	38

(III)

WORLDWIDE THREATS

THURSDAY, FEBRUARY 26, 2015

U.S. SENATE,
COMMITTEE ON ARMED SERVICES,
Washington, DC.

The committee met, pursuant to notice, at 9:34 a.m. in room SD–106, Dirksen Senate Office Building, Senator John McCain (chairman) presiding.

Committee members present: Senators McCain, Inhofe, Sessions, Wicker, Ayotte, Fischer, Cotton, Rounds, Ernst, Sullivan, Reed, Manchin, Shaheen, Gillibrand, Donnelly, Hirono, Kaine, and King.

OPENING STATEMENT OF SENATOR JOHN McCAIN, CHAIRMAN

Chairman McCAIN. Well, good morning. Good morning, everybody.

We have some nominations that, when we get sufficient number of frightened members who couldn't brave the snow today to come in—and we also have a—that——

Glad to see the Senator from Maine here, who is used to this kind of weather year-round.

So, anyway, so we'll—if we get a quorum, we'll talk about the nominations.

And also, I'd like to tell the members here that Senator Reed and I have agreed on a letter to the Budget Committee concerning our views as to what the Budget Committee should do on Defense. And, hopefully, we'll circulate that letter and get as many signatures as possible. Both Senator Reed and I have reached agreement on that letter, and I'd like you to look at it, and as many as possible can sign it.

The committee meets today to receive testimony on the nature and scope of the global threats faced by the United States and our allies.

I want to welcome James Clapper, Director of National Intelligence, and General Vincent Stewart, the newly confirmed Director of the Defense Intelligence Agency. Thank you for being with us today.

The committee recently conducted several hearings with some of our most respected national security leaders to explore the need for strategic thinking to address the threats we face. In the course of those hearings, these military and foreign policy leaders all agreed that the current international environment is more complex and dangerous than at any time in recent memory.

On the terrorism front, ISIL continues to dominate much of Syria and Iraq while spreading its dark and vicious ideology in its effort

(1)

to become the dominant Islamic extremist group in the world. At the same time, the risk of attacks by foreign fighters returning from the battlefield, or lone-wolf threats inspired by ISIL's successes, only increases the danger to the West. And Yemen, Afghanistan, Pakistan, Africa, al Qaeda and its affiliated groups continue to take advantage of ungoverned spaces to plan attacks against the United States and Western interests.

Simply put, we are engaged in a generational fight for civilization against brutal enemies, and defeating these enemies require significant intelligence resources and focus, given the diffuse and constantly evolving nature of the threat.

But, as we continue the fight against Islamic extremists, we must not lose sight of the other strategic threats we face. As the world ponders how to respond to Russia's invasion and dismemberment of Eastern Ukraine, Russia's provocations are only more worrisome in light of Vladimir Putin's intense focus on building up and modernizing Russia's military forces and doctrine and the geopolitical ambitions that these new Russian capabilities are designed to further.

In Asia, stability and security of a vital and economically significant region is threatened by North Korea's continued aggression, buildup of its nuclear arsenal, and development of long-range ballistic missiles. The far greater challenge is China's dramatic growth and modernization of its own military capabilities, which appear designed to restrict the United States military's ability to operate in the western Pacific.

That chart over there is very interesting, in that it shows the expansion by China in areas of the South China Sea. And I hope our witnesses might comment on the fact that, apparently, they are filling in enough of that area to perhaps employ weaponry such as anti-air and other capabilities.

Anyway, Iran continues to exert malign influence throughout the Middle East and Africa, using proxies in Lebanon, Syria, Iraq, Sudan, Yemen, Gaza, and Bahrain, to undermine United States strategic interests. In fact, the Iranian influence and presence in Iraq have become one of the key factors and, it seems, limitations in United States policy planning in Iraq and Syria. We must also remain focused on the myriad potential threats of the future and, thus, maintain technological superiority against potential adversaries. Today this is of most concern in the cyber and space domains, where we see increasingly capable and aggressive activities by nation-state adversaries in areas with few established norms.

I'd appreciate our witnesses' thoughts on each of these major issues. As policymakers, we look to the intelligence committee—community to provide timely and accurate information about the nature of the threats we face, the intentions of our adversaries, and the likely effect of certain actions we could take. In an age of increasing threats and flat defense budgets, the need for accurate intelligence about the plans and intentions of global actors becomes even more paramount.

Again, I want to thank Director Clapper and General Stewart for testifying today. I look forward to your assessments of the nature and scope of the myriad threats we face, how the intelligence community prioritizes and approaches these many threats, and which of these many issues concern you the most.

Senator Reed.

STATEMENT OF SENATOR JACK REED

Senator REED. Well, thank you very much, Mr. Chairman.

Let me join you in welcoming our witnesses. As they know very, very well, we currently face an alarming number of complex and varied national security challenges from many corners of the globe. And our witnesses' views on, and assessments of, these challenges are critical to the work of this committee.

Last week, I traveled to Pakistan, Afghanistan, and Iraq, and had the opportunity to meet not only with the leaders in those countries, but also with the United States civilians and uniformed personnel who are so ably and courageously serving the United States.

In Iraq, our military commanders stressed that, despite the setbacks that extremist fighters have suffered, ISIS remains capable militarily. It continues to consolidate its power in the region, including through the coercion of local populations. Coalition airstrikes have enabled local security forces, including Kurdish peshmerga and the Iraqi government's newly established militias, many of them Shi'a, to begin to gain ground from ISIS. But, concerns remain about when Iraq Security Forces will be ready to launch a counteroffensive to take Mosul and about Iran's growing influence inside Iraq. I look forward to hearing the witnesses' views on Iraq and the capabilities of both the military and the new government.

In Afghanistan and Pakistan, the Taliban remains resilient, despite coming under pressure on both sides of the border. The challenge for United States forces in Afghanistan will be to keep the counterterrorism pressure on the Taliban even as we build the capacity of Afghan Special Operations Forces to ensure that Afghanistan does not once again become a haven for al-Qaeda and other terrorists. We would be interested in our witnesses' views on the Taliban threat for the 2015 fighting season, the possibility of Pakistan-supported reconciliation talks with the Taliban and the Government of Afghanistan, and the significance of reports of a growing ISIS presence in Afghanistan and Pakistan.

On Iran, the diplomatic effort to prevent Iran's acquisition of nuclear weapons are ongoing, and the end of March is the next point at which we will assess Iran's intent with regard to its nuclear program. I hope the witnesses will provide us with an update on the intelligence community's thinking with regard to negotiations and our assessment of Iran's activities in the region under the two possible scenarios: deal or no deal.

In Syria, coalition airstrikes of the naval Kurdish fighters to regain control of Khobani and expand outward, but ISIS remains a formidable force. General Nagata will begin training the moderate Syrian opposition in the coming months. And, if successful, these forces could, over time, assist the coalition to promote the conditions for a political settlement. Just last week, at a Regional Chiefs of Defense Conference, the United States and Turkey signed a key agreement to allow training of these forces to begin in Turkey once recruits are identified. I am interested in the witnesses' views on the potential of this Syrian training initiative and the challenges we'll face.

In Europe, the post-cold-war international order is under threat from a Russia that seeks to intimidate the Ukraine and other neighboring countries through the creation or perpetuation of conflicts at increasingly aggressive military activities. Your assessment of the size of Russia's military buildup and President Putin's intentions could be of interest to the committee.

We've faced a different, but no less complex, series of challenge in the Asia-Pacific region. A recent cyber attack on Sony by North Korea illustrates the unpredictable and coercive nature of that regime and demonstrates that even a relatively small and weak rogue nation taking advantage of our unparalleled dependence on electronic networks can reach across the ocean to cause extensive damage to a United States-based economic target through cyberspace. Furthermore, while Chinese cyber attacks are not as public, they are just as problematic and continue to pose a security challenge to the United States. We would be interested to know whether we can expect more attacks of this nature and what we can do to make our systems and our Nations more resilient in the future.

Finally, we have a threat close to home, and that is sequestration. It is a threat that jeopardizes not only our National security, but our public safety, health, transportation, education, and environmental resources, as well. As we receive testimony today on the current and future threats to our National security, we here in Congress must be mindful of the necessity to find a balanced and bipartisan solution that includes a repeal of sequestration.

Thank you again for appearing today, and I look forward to hearing your testimony.

Chairman McCAIN. Welcome the witnesses.

General Clapper.

STATEMENT OF JAMES R. CLAPPER, DIRECTOR OF NATIONAL INTELLIGENCE

Mr. CLAPPER. Chairman McCain, Ranking Member Reed, and members of the committee, it's a great pleasure and honor for me to be here with General Vince Stewart. And he and I are here today to update you on some, but certainly not all, of the pressing intelligence and national security issues facing our Nation.

I need to note up front that there were some classified issues we discussed in our closed hearing on Tuesday that we won't be able to discuss as fulsomely in this open televised hearing.

In the interest of time and to allow for questions, I will only cover some of the wave tops on behalf of both of us. Two overall comments at the outset:

One, unpredictable instability is the new normal. The year 2014 saw the highest rate of political instability since 1992, the most deaths as a result of state-sponsored mass killings since the early 1990s, and the highest number of refugees and internally displaced persons, or IDPs, since World War II. Roughly half of the world's currently stable countries are at some risk of instability over the next 2 years.

The second overall comment is, this pervasive uncertainty makes it all the harder to predict the future. 2014 and 2015 saw a number of events that illustrate this difficulty: the North Korean attack on Sony, the most serious and costly cyberattack against United States interests to date, the ebola epidemic, and the small-scale but dramatic terrorist attacks in Australia, Belgium, Canada, Denmark, France, and the United States.

Again this year, I'll start with cyber threats. Attacks against us are increasing in frequency, scale, sophistication, and severity of impact. Although we must be prepared for a catastrophic large-scale strike, a so-called ''cyber Armageddon,'' the reality is that we've been living with a constant and expanding barrage of cyberattacks for some time. This insidious trend, I believe, will continue. Cyber poses a very complex set of threats, because profit-motivated criminals, ideologically motivated hackers, or extremists in variously capable nation-states, like Russia, China, North Korea, and Iran, are all potential adversaries, who, if they choose, can do great harm. Additionally, the methods of attack, the systems targeted, and the victims are also expanding in diversity and intensity on a daily basis.

2014 saw, for the first time, destructive cyberattacks carried out on United States soil by nation-state entities, marked first by the Iranian attack against the Las Vegas Sands Casino Corporation, a year ago this month, and the North Korean attack against Sony in November. While the both of these nations have lesser technical capabilities in comparison to Russia and China, these destructive attacks demonstrate that Iran and North Korea are motivated and unpredictable cyber actors.

Russia and China continue to develop very sophisticated cyber programs. While I can't go into detail here, the Russian cyber threat is more severe than we had previously assessed. And Chinese economic espionage against United States companies remains a major threat, despite detailed private-sector reports, scathing public indictments, and stern U.S. demarches.

With respect to non-nation-state entities, some ideologically motivated cyber actors expressing support for ISIL have demonstrated their capabilities by hacking several social media accounts. The so-called ''Cyber Caliphate'' successfully hacked CENTCOM's Twitter account and YouTube page in January, and, 2 weeks ago, hacked Newsweek magazine's Twitter handle.

The most pervasive cyber threat to the U.S. financial sector is from cyber criminals. Criminals were responsible for cyber intrusions in 2014 into JPMorgan, Home Depot, Target, Nieman Marcus, Anthem, and other United States companies. And, in the future, we'll probably see cyber operations that change or manipulate electronic information to compromise its integrity instead of simply deleting or disrupting access to it. In the end, the cyber threat cannot be completely eliminated. Rather, we must be vigilant in our efforts to detect, manage, and defend against it.

Moving on to terrorism. In 2013, just over 11,500 terrorist attacks worldwide killed approximately 22,000 people. Preliminary data for the first 9 months of 2014 reflects nearly 13,000 attacks, which killed 31,000 people. When the final accounting is done, 2014 will have been the most lethal year for global terrorism in the 45 years such data has been compiled. About half of all attacks, as well as fatalities, in 2014 occurred in just three countries: Iraq, Pakistan, and Afghanistan.

I'm drawing this data—the Islamic State of Iraq and the Levant (ISIL) conducted more attacks than any other terrorist group in the first 9 months of 2014, and in—credit where credit's due, I'm drawing this data from the National Consortium of the Study of Terrorism and Responses to Terrorism, or START, at the University of Maryland.

The recent terrorist attacks in Europe emphasize the threat posed by small numbers of extremists radicalized by the conflicts in Syria and Iraq. The global media attention and widespread support in extremist circles for these attacks probably will inspire additional extremists to conduct similar attacks.

And ISIL, al Qaeda, and al Qaeda in the Arabian Peninsula, and, most recently, al-Shabaab, are calling on their supporters to support lone-wolf attacks against the United States and other Western countries. Of the 13 attacks in the west since last May, 12 were conducted by individual extremists.

Since the conflict began, more than 20,000 Sunni foreign fighters have traveled to Syria from more than 90 countries to fight the Assad regime. Of that number, at least 13,600 have extremist ties. More than 3400 Western fighters have gone to Syria and Iraq. Hundreds have returned home to Europe. About 180 Americans or so have been involved in various stages of travel to Syria. I should point out this is those who've attempted to go, didn't get there, those who got there and were killed, those who got there, fought, and went to another country, and some number who have come back. A relatively small number have returned, and we've not identified any of them engaged in attack plotting. Nevertheless, the homegrown violent extremists continue to pose the most likely threat to the Homeland. Lone actors or insular groups who act autonomously will likely gravitate to simpler plots that don't require advanced skills, outside training, or communication with others. A small, but persistent, number of Sunni terrorist groups remain intent on striking the United States and the west, some of whom still see commercial aviation as an appealing target.

Moving to the Mideast, ISIL is increasing its influence outside of Iraq and Syria, seeking to expand its self-declared caliphate into the Arabian Peninsula, North Africa, and South Asia, and planning terrorist attacks against Western and Shi'a interests. ISIL's rise represents the greatest shift in the Sunni violent extremist landscape since al Qaeda affiliates first began forming, and it is the first to assume at least some characteristics of a nation-state.

Spillover from the Syrian conflict is raising the prospect of instability in Lebanon, Jordan, and Saudi Arabia. In Iraq, sectarian conflict in mixed Shi'a/Sunni areas is growing, and, if not blunted, will undermine progress against ISIL. While Prime Minister Abadi has begun to alter the ethnosectarian tone in Iraq, resistance from his Shi'a political allies and persistent distrust among Iraqi leaders will limit progress toward a stable, inclusive political environment.

ISIL's ability to conduct large-scale offensive operations in Iraq has been degraded by coalition airstrikes, the provision of weapons and munitions by the United States and other allies, and stiffened defenses by the Iraqi Security Forces, Kurdish peshmerga, Shi'a militants, and tribal allies, not to mention the Iranians. However, ISIL remains, as we've seen, a formidable and brutal threat.

Moving to Syria and parts of western Syria, the Syrian regime made consistent gains in 2014, but it will require years for it to reassert significant control of the country as a whole. The regime has a clear advantage over the opposition, which is plagued by disunity as well as firepower, manpower, and logistical shortfalls. Right now, they're incapable of militarily ousting Assad, and will probably remain so in 2015.

Assad is confident. He thinks the war is winnable. The conflict, with over 202,000 people killed—estimated to have been killed—will continue to threaten the stability of its regional neighbors and foster the rise of regional sectarianism and extremism. As well, it will strain the region's fragile economic balance as millions of refugees continue to flee the conflict. Over 52 percent of Syria's prewar population, or about 11.4 million people, has been displaced.

Iran is exerting its influence in Syria, Iraq, and Yemen. Tehran has provided robust military support to Damascus and Baghdad in the form of arms, advisors, funding, intelligence collection, electronic warfare, and cyber support, and combat support. More broadly, Iran will face many of the same decision points in 2015 as it did in 2014. Foremost is whether the Supreme Leader will agree to a nuclear deal. He wants sanctions relief, but, at the same time, to preserve his options on nuclear capabilities.

In Libya, two rival governments emerged, so the country has no clear legitimate political authority and is embroiled in a civil war. External support to both sides by countries in the region has further stoked the violence. Extremists and terrorist groups affiliated with al Qaeda and ISIL are exploiting Libya's permissive security environment. They're using the country to train and to plot. ISIL's beheadings of the Coptic Christians highlight the growing threat posed by ISIL and affiliated groups in Libya.

Moving to Yemen, the evacuation of our Embassy in Sana'a has, for now, reduced the effectiveness of our counterterrorism efforts. After President Hadi's attempted resignation and the Huthi's unilateral dissolution of the government, Yemen's political future and stability are, at best, uncertain, particularly with Hadi's apparent escape to Aden and perhaps his reassertion of his presidential authorities. Iran has provided support to the Huthis for years, and there ascendancy is increasing Iran's influence.

Let me move briefly to Russia. The crisis in Ukraine is entering its second year and is achieving—and achieving a lasting solution that allows Kiev to pursue western integration will be difficult, to say the least. Moscow sees itself in direct confrontation with the west over Ukraine, and will be very prone to overreact to United States actions. Putin's goals are to keep Ukraine out of NATO and to ensure separatist control and autonomous entity within Ukraine. He wants Moscow to retain leverage over Kiev. And Crimea, in his view, is simply not negotiable.

Russian dominance over the former Soviet space is Russia's highest foreign policy goal. Falling oil prices, Ukraine-related costs, and Western sanctions have spurred double-digit inflation and have tipped Russia's economy towards recession. Russia will continue to possess the largest, most capable foreign nuclear ballistic missile force. Russia's weapons modernization plans will focus on strategic warfare and ways to mitigate what they think are our advantages, like prompt global strike.

China. China's leaders are primarily concerned with domestic issues: the Communist Party's hold on power, internal stability, and economic growth. Although China is looking for stable ties with the United States, it's more willing to accept bilateral and regional tensions in pursuit of its interests, especially on maritime sovereignty issues. And, as you noted, Chairman McCain, China is expanding and accelerating the buildup of outposts in the South China Sea, to include stationing for their ships and potential airfields. More broadly, they continue an aggressive military modernization program directly aimed at what they consider to be our strengths. Their military training program last year included exercises unprecedented in scope, scale, and complexity to both test modernization progress and to improve their theater warfare capabilities. President Xi Jinping is pursuing an ambitious reform agenda that risks both leadership tensions and domestic unrest. The slowdown of the Chinese economy is reinforcing the leader's neuralgia about internal stability and reinforcing a harsh crackdown on internal dissent.

Needless to say, there are many more threats to United States interests worldwide that we can address, many of which are covered in detail in our statement for the record—notably, the classified version—such as Afghanistan, North Korea, and weapons of mass destruction.

But, I think, with that grim litany, will—I will stop and will open to your questions.

[The prepared statement of Mr. Clapper follows:]

Statement for the Record

Worldwide Threat Assessment
of the
US Intelligence Community

Senate Armed Services Committee

James R. Clapper

Director of National Intelligence

February 26, 2015

STATEMENT FOR THE RECORD

WORLDWIDE THREAT ASSESSMENT
of the
US INTELLIGENCE COMMUNITY

February 26, 2015

INTRODUCTION

Chairman McCain, Ranking Member Reed, Members of the Committee, thank you for the invitation to offer the United States Intelligence Community's 2015 assessment of threats to US national security. My statement reflects the collective insights of the Intelligence Community's extraordinary men and women, whom I am privileged and honored to lead. We in the Intelligence Community are committed every day to provide the nuanced, multidisciplinary intelligence that policymakers, warfighters, and domestic law enforcement personnel need to protect American lives and America's interests anywhere in the world.

Information available as of February 13, 2015 was used in the preparation of this assessment.

TABLE OF CONTENTS

Page

GLOBAL THREATS

Cyber	1
Counterintelligence	4
Terrorism	4
Weapons of Mass Destruction and Proliferation	5
Space and Counterspace	7
Transnational Organized Crime	8
Economics and Natural Resources	9
Human Security	10

REGIONAL THREATS

Middle East and North Africa	13
Iraq	13
Syria	13
Islamic State of Iraq and the Levant	14
Iran	14
Libya	15
Yemen	15
Lebanon	15
Egypt	16
Tunisia	16
Europe	16
Turkey	16
Key Partners	17
Russia and Eurasia	17
Russia	17
Ukraine, Moldova, and Belarus	18
The Caucasus and Central Asia	19

12

East Asia 19
    China 19
    North Korea 20

South Asia 20
    Afghanistan 20
    Pakistan 21
    India 21

Sub-Saharan Africa 22
    West Africa 22
    Sudan 22
    South Sudan 22
    Nigeria 23
    Somalia 23
    Lord's Resistance Army 23
    Central African Republic 23
    The Sahel 23

Latin America and the Caribbean 24
    Cuba 24
    Central America 24
    Venezuela 24
    Haiti 25

GLOBAL THREATS

CYBER

Strategic Assessment

Cyber threats to US national and economic security are increasing in frequency, scale, sophistication, and severity of impact. The ranges of cyber threat actors, methods of attack, targeted systems, and victims are also expanding. Overall, the unclassified information and communication technology (ICT) networks that support US Government, military, commercial, and social activities remain vulnerable to espionage and/or disruption. However, the likelihood of a catastrophic attack from any particular actor is remote at this time. Rather than a "Cyber Armageddon" scenario that debilitates the entire US infrastructure, we envision something different. We foresee an ongoing series of low-to-moderate level cyber attacks from a variety of sources over time, which will impose cumulative costs on US economic competitiveness and national security.

- A growing number of computer forensic studies by industry experts strongly suggest that several nations—including Iran and North Korea—have undertaken offensive cyber operations against private sector targets to support their economic and foreign policy objectives, at times concurrent with political crises.

Risk. Despite ever-improving network defenses, the diverse possibilities for remote hacking intrusions, supply chain operations to insert compromised hardware or software, and malevolent activities by human insiders will hold nearly all ICT systems at risk for years to come. In short, the cyber threat cannot be eliminated; rather, cyber risk must be managed. Moreover, the risk calculus employed by some private sector entities does not adequately account for foreign cyber threats or the systemic interdependencies between different critical infrastructure sectors.

Costs. During 2014, we saw an increase in the scale and scope of reporting on malevolent cyber activity that can be measured by the amount of corporate data stolen or deleted, personally identifiable information (PII) compromised, or remediation costs incurred by US victims. For example:

- After the 2012-13 distributed denial of service (DDOS) attacks on the US financial sector, JPMorgan Chase (JPMorgan) announced plans for annual cyber security expenditures of $250 million by the end of 2014. After the company suffered a hacking intrusion in 2014, JPMorgan's CEO said he would probably double JPMorgan's annual computer security budget within the next five years.

- The 2014 data breach at Home Depot exposed information from 56 million credit/debit cards and 53 million customer email addresses. Home Depot estimated the cost of the breach to be $62 million.

- In 2014, unauthorized computer intrusions were detected on the networks of the Office of Personnel Management (OPM) as well as its contractors, US Investigations Services (USIS) and KeyPoint

Government Solutions. The two contractors were involved in processing sensitive PII related to national security clearances for Federal Government employees.

- In August 2014, the US company, Community Health Systems, informed the Securities and Exchange Commission that it believed hackers "originating from China" had stolen PII on 4.5 million individuals.

Attribution. Although cyber operators can infiltrate or disrupt targeted ICT networks, most can no longer assume that their activities will remain undetected. Nor can they assume that if detected, they will be able to conceal their identities. Governmental and private sector security professionals have made significant advances in detecting and attributing cyber intrusions.

- In May 2014, the US Department of Justice indicted five officers from China's Peoples' Liberation Army on charges of hacking US companies.

- In December 2014, computer security experts reported that members of an Iranian organization were responsible for computer operations targeting US military, transportation, public utility, and other critical infrastructure networks.

Deterrence. Numerous actors remain undeterred from conducting economic cyber espionage or perpetrating cyber attacks. The absence of universally accepted and enforceable norms of behavior in cyberspace has contributed to this situation. The motivation to conduct cyber attacks and cyber espionage will probably remain strong because of the relative ease of these operations and the gains they bring to the perpetrators. The result is a cyber environment in which multiple actors continue to test their adversaries' technical capabilities, political resolve, and thresholds. The muted response by most victims to cyber attacks has created a permissive environment in which low-level attacks can be used as a coercive tool short of war, with relatively low risk of retaliation. Additionally, even when a cyber attack can be attributed to a specific actor, the forensic attribution often requires a significant amount of time to complete. Long delays between the cyber attack and determination of attribution likewise reinforce a permissive environment.

Threat Actors

Politically motivated cyber attacks are now a growing reality, and foreign actors are reconnoitering and developing access to US critical infrastructure systems, which might be quickly exploited for disruption if an adversary's intent became hostile. In addition, those conducting cyber espionage are targeting US government, military, and commercial networks on a daily basis. These threats come from a range of actors, including: (1) nation states with highly sophisticated cyber programs (such as Russia or China), (2) nations with lesser technical capabilities but possibly more disruptive intent (such as Iran or North Korea), (3) profit-motivated criminals, and (4) ideologically motivated hackers or extremists. Distinguishing between state and non-state actors within the same country is often difficult—especially when those varied actors actively collaborate, tacitly cooperate, condone criminal activity that only harms foreign victims, or utilize similar cyber tools.

Russia. Russia's Ministry of Defense is establishing its own cyber command, which—according to senior Russian military officials—will be responsible for conducting offensive cyber activities, including propaganda operations and inserting malware into enemy command and control systems. Russia's armed forces are also establishing a specialized branch for computer network operations.

* Computer security studies assert that unspecified Russian cyber actors are developing means to access industrial control systems (ICS) remotely. These systems manage critical infrastructures such as electric power grids, urban mass-transit systems, air-traffic control, and oil and gas distribution networks. These unspecified Russian actors have successfully compromised the product supply chains of three ICS vendors so that customers download exploitative malware directly from the vendors' websites along with routine software updates, according to private sector cyber security experts.

China. Chinese economic espionage against US companies remains a significant issue. The "advanced persistent threat" activities continue despite detailed private sector reports, public indictments, and US demarches, according to a computer security study. China is an advanced cyber actor; however, Chinese hackers often use less sophisticated cyber tools to access targets. Improved cyber defenses would require hackers to use more sophisticated skills and make China's economic espionage more costly and difficult to conduct.

Iran. Iran very likely values its cyber program as one of many tools for carrying out asymmetric but proportional retaliation against political foes, as well as a sophisticated means of collecting intelligence. Iranian actors have been implicated in the 2012-13 DDOS attacks against US financial institutions and in the February 2014 cyber attack on the Las Vegas Sands casino company.

North Korea. North Korea is another state actor that uses its cyber capabilities for political objectives. The North Korean Government was responsible for the November 2014 cyber attack on Sony Pictures Entertainment (SPE), which stole corporate information and introduced hard drive erasing malware into the company's network infrastructure, according to the FBI. The attack coincided with the planned release of a SPE feature film satire that depicted the planned assassination of the North Korean president.

Terrorists. Terrorist groups will continue to experiment with hacking, which could serve as the foundation for developing more advanced capabilities. Terrorist sympathizers will probably conduct low-level cyber attacks on behalf of terrorist groups and attract attention of the media, which might exaggerate the capabilities and threat posed by these actors.

Integrity of Information

Most of the public discussion regarding cyber threats has focused on the confidentiality and availability of information; cyber espionage undermines confidentiality, whereas denial-of-service operations and data-deletion attacks undermine availability. In the future, however, we might also see more cyber operations that will change or manipulate electronic information in order to compromise its integrity (i.e. accuracy and reliability) instead of deleting it or disrupting access to it. Decisionmaking by senior government officials (civilian and military), corporate executives, investors, or others will be impaired if they cannot trust the information they are receiving.

- Successful cyber operations targeting the integrity of information would need to overcome any institutionalized checks and balances designed to prevent the manipulation of data, for example, market monitoring and clearing functions in the financial sector.

COUNTERINTELLIGENCE

We assess that the leading state intelligence threats to US interests in 2015 will continue to be Russia and China, based on their capabilities, intent, and broad operational scopes. Other states in South Asia, the Near East, and East Asia will pose increasingly sophisticated local and regional intelligence threats to US interests. For example, Iran's intelligence and security services continue to view the United States as a primary threat and have stated publicly that they monitor and counter US activities in the region.

Penetrating the US national decisionmaking apparatus and Intelligence Community will remain primary objectives for foreign intelligence entities. Additionally, the targeting of national security information and proprietary information from US companies and research institutions dealing with defense, energy, finance, dual-use technology, and other areas will be a persistent threat to US interests.

Non-state entities, including transnational organized criminals and terrorists, will continue to employ human, technical, and cyber intelligence capabilities that present a significant counterintelligence challenge. Like state intelligence services, these non-state entities recruit sources and perform physical and technical surveillance to facilitate their illegal activities and avoid detection and capture.

The internationalization of critical US supply chains and service infrastructure, including for the ICT, civil infrastructure, and national security sectors, increases the potential for subversion. This threat includes individuals, small groups of "hacktivists," commercial firms, and state intelligence services

Trusted insiders who disclose sensitive US Government information without authorization will remain a significant threat in 2015. The technical sophistication and availability of information technology that can be used for nefarious purposes exacerbates this threat.

TERRORISM

Sunni violent extremists are gaining momentum and the number of Sunni violent extremist groups, members, and safe havens is greater than at any other point in history. These groups challenge local and regional governance and threaten US allies, partners, and interests. The threat to key US allies and partners will probably increase, but the extent of the increase will depend on the level of success that Sunni violent extremists achieve in seizing and holding territory whether or not attacks on local regimes and calls for retaliation against the West are accepted by their key audiences, and the durability of the US-led coalition in Iraq and Syria.

Sunni violent extremists have taken advantage of fragile or unstable Muslim-majority countries to make territorial advances, seen in Syria and Iraq, and will probably continue to do so. They also contribute to regime instability and internal conflict by engaging in high levels of violence. Most will be unable to seize and hold territory on a large scale, however, as long as local, regional, and international support and resources are available and dedicated to halting their progress. The increase in the number of Sunni violent extremist groups also will probably be balanced by a lack of cohesion and authoritative leadership. Although the January 2015 attacks against Charlie Hebdo in Paris is a reminder of the threat to the West, most groups place a higher priority on local concerns than on attacking the so-called far enemy—the United States and the West—as advocated by core al-Qa'ida.

Differences in ideology and tactics will foster competition among some of these groups, particularly if a unifying figure or group does not emerge. In some cases, groups—even if hostile to each other— will ally against common enemies. For example, some Sunni violent extremists will probably gain support from like-minded insurgent or anti-regime groups or within disaffected or disenfranchised communities because they share the goal of radical regime change.

Although most homegrown violent extremists (HVEs) will probably continue to aspire to travel overseas, particularly to Syria and Iraq, they will probably remain the most likely Sunni violent extremist threat to the US homeland because of their immediate and direct access. Some might have been inspired by calls by the Islamic State of Iraq and the Levant (ISIL) in late September for individual jihadists in the West to retaliate for US-led airstrikes on ISIL. Attacks by lone actors are among the most difficult to warn about because they offer few or no signatures.

If ISIL were to substantially increase the priority it places on attacking the West rather than fighting to maintain and expand territorial control, then the group's access to radicalized Westerners who have fought in Syria and Iraq would provide a pool of operatives who potentially have access to the United States and other Western countries. Since the conflict began in 2011, more than 20,000 foreign fighters—at least 3,400 of whom are Westerners—have gone to Syria from more than 90 countries.

WEAPONS OF MASS DESTRUCTION AND PROLIFERATION

Nation-states' efforts to develop or acquire weapons of mass destruction (WMD), their delivery systems, or their underlying technologies constitute a major threat to the security of the United States, its deployed troops, and allies. Syrian regime use of chemical weapons against the opposition further demonstrates that the threat of WMD is real. The time when only a few states had access to the most dangerous technologies is past. Biological and chemical materials and technologies, almost always dual-use, move easily in the globalized economy, as do personnel with the scientific expertise to design and use them. The latest discoveries in the life sciences also diffuse rapidly around the globe.

Iran Preserving Nuclear Weapons Option

We continue to assess that Iran's overarching strategic goals of enhancing its security, prestige, and regional influence have led it to pursue capabilities to meet its civilian goals and give it the ability to build missile-deliverable nuclear weapons, if it chooses to do so. We do not know whether Iran will eventually decide to build nuclear weapons.

We also continue to assess that Iran does not face any insurmountable technical barriers to producing a nuclear weapon, making Iran's political will the central issue. However, Iranian implementation of the Joint Plan of Action (JPOA) has at least temporarily inhibited further progress in its uranium enrichment and plutonium production capabilities and effectively eliminated Iran's stockpile of 20 percent enriched uranium. The agreement has also enhanced the transparency of Iran's nuclear activities, mainly through improved International Atomic Energy Agency (IAEA) access and earlier warning of any effort to make material for nuclear weapons using its safeguarded facilities.

We judge that Tehran would choose ballistic missiles as its preferred method of delivering nuclear weapons, if it builds them. Iran's ballistic missiles are inherently capable of delivering WMD, and Tehran already has the largest inventory of ballistic missiles in the Middle East. Iran's progress on space launch vehicles—along with its desire to deter the United States and its allies—provides Tehran with the means and motivation to develop longer-range missiles, including intercontinental ballistic missiles (ICBMs).

North Korea Developing WMD-Applicable Capabilities

North Korea's nuclear weapons and missile programs pose a serious threat to the United States and to the security environment in East Asia. North Korea's export of ballistic missiles and associated materials to several countries, including Iran and Syria, and its assistance to Syria's construction of a nuclear reactor, destroyed in 2007, illustrate its willingness to proliferate dangerous technologies.

In 2013, following North Korea's third nuclear test, Pyongyang announced its intention to "refurbish and restart" its nuclear facilities, to include the uranium enrichment facility at Yongbyon, and to restart its graphite-moderated plutonium production reactor that was shut down in 2007. We assess that North Korea has followed through on its announcement by expanding its Yongbyon enrichment facility and restarting the reactor.

North Korea has also expanded the size and sophistication of its ballistic missile forces, ranging from close-range ballistic missiles to ICBMs, while continuing to conduct test launches. In 2014, North Korea launched an unprecedented number of ballistic missiles.

Pyongyang is committed to developing a long-range, nuclear-armed missile that is capable of posing a direct threat to the United States and has publicly displayed its KN08 road-mobile ICBM twice. We assess that North Korea has already taken initial steps toward fielding this system, although the system has not been flight-tested.

Because of deficiencies in their conventional military forces, North Korean leaders are focused on developing missile and WMD capabilities, particularly building nuclear weapons. Although North Korean state media regularly carries official statements on North Korea's justification for building nuclear weapons and threatening to use them as a defensive or retaliatory measure, we do not know the details of Pyongyang's nuclear doctrine or employment concepts. We have long assessed that, in Pyongyang's view, its nuclear capabilities are intended for deterrence, international prestige, and coercive diplomacy.

China's Expanding Nuclear Forces

The People's Liberation Army's (PLA's) Second Artillery Force continues to modernize its nuclear missile force by adding more survivable road-mobile systems and enhancing its silo-based systems. This new generation of missiles is intended to ensure the viability of China's strategic deterrent by providing a second strike capability. In addition, the PLA Navy continues to develop the JL-2 submarine-launched ballistic missile (SLBM) and might produce additional JIN-class nuclear-powered ballistic missile submarines. The JIN-class submarines, armed with JL-2 SLBMs, will give the PLA Navy its first long-range, sea-based nuclear capability. We assess that the Navy will soon conduct its first nuclear deterrence patrols.

Russia's New Intermediate-Range Cruise Missile

Russia has developed a new cruise missile that the United States has declared to be in violation of the Intermediate-Range Nuclear Forces (INF) Treaty. In 2013, Sergei Ivanov, a senior Russian administration official, commented in an interview how the world had changed since the time the INF Treaty was signed 1987 and noted that Russia was "developing appropriate weapons systems" in light of the proliferation of intermediate- and shorter-range ballistic missile technologies around the world. Similarly, as far back as 2007, Ivanov publicly announced that Russia had tested a ground-launched cruise missile for its Iskander weapon system, whose range complied with the INF Treaty "for now." The development of a cruise missile that is inconsistent with INF, combined with these statements about INF, calls into question Russia's commitment to this treaty.

WMD Security in Syria

In June 2014, Syria's declared CW stockpile was removed for destruction by the international community. The most hazardous chemical agents were destroyed aboard the MV CAPE RAY as of August 2014. The United States and its allies continue to work closely with the Organization for the Prohibition of Chemical Weapons (OPCW) to verify the completeness and accuracy of Syria's Chemical Weapons Convention (CWC) declaration. We judge that Syria, despite signing the treaty, has used chemicals as a means of warfare since accession to the CWC in 2013. Furthermore, the OPCW continues to investigate allegations of chlorine use in Syria.

SPACE AND COUNTERSPACE

Threats to US space systems and services will increase during 2015 and beyond as potential adversaries pursue disruptive and destructive counterspace capabilities. Chinese and Russian military leaders understand the unique information advantages afforded by space systems and services and are developing capabilities to deny access in a conflict. Chinese military writings highlight the need to interfere with, damage, and destroy reconnaissance, navigation, and communication satellites. China has satellite jamming capabilities and is pursuing antisatellite systems. In July 2014, China conducted a non-destructive antisatellite missile test. China conducted a previous destructive test of the system in 2007, which created long-lived space debris. Russia's 2010 Military Doctrine emphasizes space defense as a vital component of its national defense. Russian leaders openly assert that the Russian armed forces have antisatellite weapons and conduct antisatellite research. Russia has satellite jammers and is pursuing antisatellite systems.

TRANSNATIONAL ORGANIZED CRIME

Transnational Organized Crime (TOC) is a global, persistent threat to our communities at home and our interests abroad. Savvy, profit-driven criminal networks traffic in drugs, persons, wildlife, and weapons; corrode security and governance; undermine legitimate economic activity and the rule of law; cost economies important revenue; and undercut US development efforts.

Drug Trafficking

Drug trafficking will remain a major TOC threat to the United States. Mexico is the largest foreign producer of US-bound marijuana, methamphetamines, and heroin, and the conduit for the overwhelming majority of US-bound cocaine from South America. The drug trade also undermines US interests abroad, eroding stability in parts of Africa and Latin America; Afghanistan accounts for 80 percent of the world's opium production. Weak Central American states will continue to be the primary transit area for the majority of US-bound cocaine. The Caribbean is becoming an increasingly important secondary transit area for US- and European-bound cocaine. In 2013, the world's capacity to produce heroin reached the second highest level in nearly 20 years, increasing the likelihood that the drug will remain accessible and inexpensive in consumer markets in the United States, where heroin-related deaths have surged since 2007. New psychoactive substances (NPS), including synthetic cannabinoids and synthetic cathinones, pose an emerging and rapidly growing global public health threat. Since 2009, US law enforcement officials have encountered more than 240 synthetic compounds. Worldwide, 348 new psychoactive substances had been identified, exceeding the number of 234 illicit substances under international controls.

Criminals Profiting from Global Instability

Transnational criminal organizations will continue to exploit opportunities in ongoing conflicts to destabilize societies, economies, and governance. Regional unrest, population displacements, endemic corruption, and political turmoil will provide openings that criminals will exploit for profit and to improve their standing relative to other power brokers.

Corruption

Corruption facilitates transnational organized crime and vice versa. Both phenomena exacerbate other threats to local, regional, and international security. Corruption exists at some level in all countries; however, the symbiotic relationship between government officials and TOC networks is particularly pernicious in some countries. One example is Russia, where the nexus among organized crime, state actors, and business blurs the distinction between state policy and private gain.

Human Trafficking

Human trafficking remains both a human rights concern and a challenge to international security. Trafficking in persons has become a lucrative source of revenue—estimated to produce tens of billions of dollars annually. Human traffickers leverage corrupt officials, porous borders, and lax enforcement to ply their illicit trade. This exploitation of human lives for profit continues to occur in every country in the world—undermining the rule of law and corroding legitimate institutions of government and commerce.

Wildlife Trafficking

Illicit trade in wildlife, timber, and marine resources endangers the environment, threatens rule of law and border security in fragile regions, and destabilizes communities that depend on wildlife for biodiversity and ecotourism. Increased demand for ivory and rhino horn in Asia has triggered unprecedented increases in poaching in Africa. Criminal elements, often in collusion with corrupt government officials or security forces, are involved in poaching and movement of ivory and rhino horn across Africa. Poaching presents significant security challenges for militaries and police forces in African nations, which often are outgunned by poachers and their allies. Illegal, unreported, and unregulated fishing threatens food security and the preservation of marine resources. It often occurs concurrently with forced labor in the fishing industry.

Theft of Cultural Properties, Artifacts, and Antiquities

Although the theft and trafficking of cultural heritage and art are traditions as old as the cultures they represent, transnational organized criminals are acquiring, transporting, and selling valuable cultural property and art more swiftly, easily, and stealthily. These criminals operate on a global scale without regard for laws, borders, nationalities or the significance of the treasures they smuggle.

ECONOMICS AND NATURAL RESOURCES

The global economy continues to adjust to and recover from the global financial crisis that began in 2008; economic growth since that period is lagging behind that of the previous decade. Resumption of sustained growth has been elusive for many of the world's largest economies, particularly in European countries and Japan. The prospect of diminished or forestalled recoveries in these developed economies as well as disappointing growth in key developing countries has contributed to a readjustment of energy and commodity markets.

Energy and Commodities

Energy prices experienced sharp declines during the second half of 2014. Diminishing global growth prospects, OPEC's decision to maintain its output levels, rapid increases in unconventional oil production in Canada and the United States, and the partial resumption of some previously sidelined output in Libya and elsewhere helped drive down prices by more than half since July, the first substantial decline since 2008-09. Lower-priced oil and gas will give a boost to the global economy, with benefits enjoyed by importers more than outweighing the costs to exporters.

Macroeconomic Stability

Extraordinary monetary policy or "quantitative easing" has helped revive growth in the United States since the global financial crisis. However, this recovery and the prospect of higher returns in the United States will probably continue to draw investment capital from the rest of the world, where weak growth has left interest rates depressed.

Global output improved slightly in 2014 but continued to lag the growth rates seen before 2008. Since 2008, the worldwide GDP growth rate has averaged about 3.2 percent, well below its 20-year, pre-GFC average of 3.9 percent. Looking ahead, prospects for slowing economic growth in Europe and China do not bode well for the global economic environment.

Economic growth has been inconsistent among developed and developing economies alike. Outside of the largest economies—the United States, the EU, and China—economic growth largely stagnated worldwide in 2014, slowing to 2.1 percent. As a result, the difference in growth rates of developing countries and developed countries continued to narrow—to 2.6 percentage points. This gap, smallest in more than a decade, underscores the continued weakness in emerging markets, whose previously much-higher average growth rates helped drive global growth.

HUMAN SECURITY

Critical Trends Converging

Several trends are converging that will probably increase the frequency of shocks to human security in 2015. Emerging infectious diseases and deficiencies in international state preparedness to address them remain a threat, exemplified by the epidemic spread of the Ebola virus in West Africa. Extremes in weather combined with public policies that affect food and water supplies will probably exacerbate humanitarian crises. Many states and international institutions will look to the United States in 2015 for leadership to address human security issues, particularly environment and global health, as well as those caused by poor or abusive governance.

Global trends in governance are negative and portend growing instability. Poor and abusive governance threatens the security and rights of individuals and civil society in many countries throughout the world. The overall risk for mass atrocities—driven in part by increasing social mobilization, violent conflict, and a diminishing quality of governance—is growing. Incidents of religious persecution also are on the rise. Legal restrictions on NGOs and the press, particularly those that expose government shortcomings or lobby for reforms, will probably continue.

Infectious Disease Continues To Threaten Human Security Worldwide

Infectious diseases are among the foremost health security threats. A more crowded and interconnected world is increasing the opportunities for human and animal diseases to emerge and spread globally. This has been demonstrated by the emergence of Ebola in West Africa on an unprecedented scale. In addition, military conflicts and displacement of populations with loss of basic infrastructure can lead to spread of disease. Climate change can also lead to changes in the distribution of vectors for diseases.

- The Ebola outbreak, which began in late 2013 in a remote area of Guinea, quickly spread into neighboring Liberia and Sierra Leone and then into dense urban transportation hubs, where it began spreading out of control. Gaps in disease surveillance and reporting, limited health care resources, and other factors contributed to the outpacing of the international community's response in West Africa. Isolated Ebola cases appeared outside of the most affected countries—notably in Spain and the United States—and the disease will almost certainly continue in 2015 to threaten regional economic stability, security, and governance.

- Antimicrobial drug resistance is increasingly threatening global health security. Seventy percent of known bacteria have acquired resistance to at least one antibiotic that is used to treat infections, threatening a return to the pre-antibiotic era. Multidrug-resistant tuberculosis has emerged in China, India, Russia, and elsewhere. During the next twenty years antimicrobial drug-resistant pathogens will probably continue to increase in number and geographic scope, worsening health outcomes, straining public health budgets, and harming US interests throughout the world.

- MERS, a novel virus from the same family as SARS, emerged in 2012 in Saudi Arabia. Isolated cases migrated to Southeast Asia, Europe, and the United States. Cases of highly pathogenic influenza are also continuing to appear in different regions of the world. HIV/AIDS and malaria, although trending downward, remain global health priorities. In 2013, 2.1 million people were newly infected with HIV and 584,000 were killed by malaria, according to the World Health Organization. Diarrheal diseases like cholera continue to take the lives of 800,000 children annually.

- The world's population remains vulnerable to infectious diseases because anticipating which pathogen might spread from animals to humans or if a human virus will take a more virulent form is nearly impossible. For example, if a highly pathogenic avian influenza virus like H7N9 were to become easily transmissible among humans, the outcome could be far more disruptive than the great influenza pandemic of 1918. It could lead to global economic losses, the unseating of governments, and disturbance of geopolitical alliances.

Extreme Weather Exacerbating Risks to Global Food and Water Security

Extreme weather, climate change, and public policies that affect food and water supplies will probably create or exacerbate humanitarian crises and instability risks. Globally averaged surface temperature rose approximately 0.6 degrees Celsius (about 1.4 degrees Fahrenheit) from 1951 to 2014; 2014 was warmest on earth since recordkeeping began. This rise in temperature has probably caused an increase in the intensity and frequency of both heavy precipitation and prolonged heat waves and has changed the spread of certain diseases. This trend will probably continue. Demographic and development trends that concentrate people in cities—often along coasts—will compound and amplify the impact of extreme weather and climate change on populations. Countries whose key systems—food, water, energy, shelter, transportation, and medical—are resilient will be better able to avoid significant economic and human losses from extreme weather.

- Global food supplies will probably be adequate for 2015 but are becoming increasingly fragile in Africa, the Middle East, and South Asia. The risks of worsening food insecurity in regions of strategic importance to the United States will increase because of threats to local food availability, lower purchasing power, and counterproductive government policies. Price shocks will result if extreme weather or disease patterns significantly reduce food production in multiple areas of the world, especially in key exporting countries.

- Risks to freshwater supplies—due to shortages, poor quality, floods, and climate change—are growing. These problems hinder the ability of countries to produce food and generate energy, potentially undermining global food markets and hobbling economic growth. Combined with demographic and economic development pressures, such problems will particularly hinder the efforts of North Africa, the Middle East, and South Asia to cope with their water problems. Lack of adequate water might be a destabilizing factor in countries that lack the management mechanisms, financial resources, political will, or technical ability to solve their internal water problems.

- Some states are heavily dependent on river water controlled by upstream nations. When upstream water infrastructure development threatens downstream access to water, states might attempt to exert pressure on their neighbors to preserve their water interests. Such pressure might be applied in international forums and also includes pressing investors, nongovernmental organizations, and donor countries to support or halt water infrastructure projects. Some countries will almost certainly construct and support major water projects. Over the longer term, wealthier developing countries will also probably face increasing water-related social disruptions. Developing countries, however, are almost certainly capable of addressing water problems without risk of state failure. Terrorist organizations might also increasingly seek to control or degrade water infrastructure to gain revenue or influence populations.

Increase in Global Instability Risk

Global political instability risks will remain high in 2015 and beyond. Mass atrocities, sectarian or religious violence, and curtailed NGO activities will all continue to increase these risks. Declining economic conditions are contributing to risk of instability or internal conflict.

- Roughly half of the world's countries not already experiencing or recovering from instability are in the "most risk" and "significant risk" categories for regime-threatening and violent instability through 2015.

- Overall international will and capability to prevent or mitigate mass atrocities will probably diminish in 2015 owing to reductions in government budgets and spending.

- In 2014, about two dozen countries increased restrictions on NGOs. Approximately another dozen also plan to do so in 2015, according to the International Center for Nonprofit Law.

REGIONAL THREATS

MIDDLE EAST AND NORTH AFRICA

Iraq

Over six months into the coalition campaign against the Islamic State of Iraq and the Levant (ISIL), the frontlines against the group in Iraq have largely stabilized; no side is able to muster the resources necessary to attain its territorial ambitions. The Iraqi Security Forces (ISF), Peshmerga, Shia militants, and a few tribal allies—bolstered by air and artillery strikes, weapons, and advice from the United States, Arab and Western allies, and Iran—have prevented ISIL from gaining large swaths of additional territory.

Sectarian conflict in mixed Shia-Sunni areas in and around Baghdad that can undermine progress against ISIL is growing. ISF and Shia militants are conducting a campaign of retribution killings and forced displacement of Sunni civilians in several areas contested by Sunni militants.

Since taking office, Prime Minister al-Abadi has taken steps to change the ethno-sectarian tone in Baghdad, including engaging Sunni tribal leaders and reaching a tentative oil agreement with the Kurdistan Regional Government. However, the ethnosectarian nature of security operations and persistent distrust among Iraqi leaders risk undermining Abadi's nascent political progress.

Syria

The Syrian regime made consistent gains in 2014 in parts of western Syria that it considers key, retaking ground in eastern Damascus, Homs, and Latakia; it is close to surrounding Aleppo city. The regime will require years to reassert significant control over the country.

- The bulk of the opposition in the north is fighting on three fronts—against the regime, the al-Qa'ida-affiliated Nusrah Front, and ISIL. The opposition in the south has made steady gains in areas that the regime has not made a priority and where ISIL has only a limited presence.

The stability of Syria's neighbors is at risk due to the country's prolonged conflict, which will strain regional economies forced to absorb millions of refugees. The conflict will also encourage regional sectarianism and continue to incubate extremist groups that will use Syria as a launching pad for attacks across the Middle East.

- The Syrian conflict is also putting huge economic and resource strains on countries in the region primarily due to the nearly 4 million refugees fleeing the conflict. Most of the refugees have fled to neighboring states. More than 620,000 are in Jordan; almost 1.6 million are in Turkey; almost 1.2 million are in Lebanon; and more than 240,000 are in Iraq. These states have requested additional international support to manage the influx.

Islamic State of Iraq and the Levant

In an attempt to strengthen its self-declared caliphate, ISIL probably plans to conduct operations against regional allies, Western facilities, and personnel in the Middle East; it has already executed Western and Japanese hostages as well as a Jordanian Air Force pilot. ISIL leader Abu Bakr al-Baghdadi outlined the group's ambitious external goals, including the expansion of the caliphate into the Arabian Peninsula and North Africa and attacks against Western, regional, and Shia interests, according to a public statement in November 2014.

- In September 2014, ISIL publicly called on all Sunnis to retaliate for US-led airstrikes in Iraq and Syria, advocating the targeting of law enforcement and other government officials using any means available. Individuals from Europe and North America who have trained and fought with ISIL can return home and conduct attacks either on their own or on ISIL's behalf. The French citizen arrested in May 2014 for a shooting at a Jewish museum in Brussels had returned from fighting, probably with ISIL in Syria, and was wrapped in a flag with ISIL inscriptions when he was apprehended. We do not know whether he acted at ISIL's behest.

Iran

The Islamic Republic of Iran is an ongoing threat to US national interests because of its support to the Asad regime in Syria, promulgation of anti-Israeli policies, development of advanced military capabilities, and pursuit of its nuclear program. President Ruhani—a longstanding member of the regime establishment—will not depart from Iran's national security objectives of protecting the regime and enhancing Iranian influence abroad, even while attempting different approaches to achieve these goals. He requires Supreme Leader Khamenei's support to continue engagement with the West, moderate foreign policy, and ease social restrictions within Iran.

Iran possesses a substantial inventory of theater ballistic missiles capable of reaching as far as some areas of southeastern Europe. Tehran is developing increasingly sophisticated missiles and improving the range and accuracy of its other missile systems. Iran is also acquiring advanced naval and aerospace capabilities, including naval mines, small but capable submarines, coastal defense cruise missile batteries, attack craft, anti-ship missiles, and armed unmanned aerial vehicles.

In Iraq and Syria, Iran seeks to preserve friendly governments, protect Shia interests, defeat Sunni extremists, and marginalize US influence. The rise of ISIL has prompted Iran to devote more resources to blunting Sunni extremist advances that threaten Iran's regional allies and interests. Iran's security services have provided robust military support to Baghdad and Damascus, including arms, advisers, funding, and direct combat support. Both conflicts have allowed Iran to gain valuable on-the-ground experience in counterinsurgency operations. Iranian assistance has been instrumental in expanding the capabilities of Shia militants in Iraq. The ISIL threat has also reduced Iraqi resistance to integrating those militants, with Iranian help, into the Iraqi Security Forces, but Iran has uneven control over these groups.

Despite Iran's intentions to dampen sectarianism, build responsive partners, and deescalate tensions with Saudi Arabia, Iranian leaders—particularly within the security services—are pursuing policies with negative secondary consequences for regional stability and potentially for Iran. Iran's actions to protect and empower Shia communities are fueling growing fears and sectarian responses.

Libya

We assess that Libya will remain volatile in 2015. Political polarization and broadening militia violence have pushed Libya into a civil war. Nearly four years since the revolution that toppled Qadhafi, rival governments have emerged, leaving the country with no clear legitimate political authority or credible security forces. Militias aligned with the rival governments continue to vie for dominance in Tripoli and Benghazi.

* In Benghazi, fighting that began in May 2014 is ongoing between forces aligned with former General Khalifa Hafar's Operation Dignity forces and Ansar al-Sharia (AAS) and allied groups. In Tripoli, the Libya Dawn militias have driven their Zintani militia rivals out of the city, but fighting continues southwest of Tripoli.

* UN efforts to facilitate a negotiated resolution between Libya's rival governments have shown limited momentum but as of early February 2015 have not made tangible progress toward a unity government or a durable cease-fire.

Extremists and terrorists from al-Qa'ida-affiliated and allied groups are using Libya's permissive security environment as a safe haven to plot attacks, including against Western interests in Libya and the region. ISIL also has declared the country part of its caliphate, and ISIL-aligned extremists are trying to institute *sharia* in parts of the country.

Yemen

The Huthis have emerged as the most powerful group in Yemen since taking Sanaa last fall and are poised to dominate the political process after President's Hadi's resignation and their dissolution of the government. The group, however, continues to face resistance as it expands toward the south and east. Southern Yemeni leaders have been alarmed by the Huthi's consolidation of control in Sanaa and are poised to oppose further Huthi expansion south. Al-Qa'ida in the Arabian Peninsula (AQAP) has taken advantage of many Sunni tribes' opposition to Huthi expansion to gain recruits to fight against the Huthis.

Chronic and severe economic and humanitarian problems, exacerbated by repeated pipeline attacks and the Huthis' push to reinstate costly fuel subsidies, will continue to undercut government control and legitimacy. Yemen will probably continue pressuring donor nations to make good on aid pledges while negotiating with tribes outside of Sanaa's control to keep oil exports flowing.

Huthi ascendency in Yemen has increased Iran's influence as well.

Lebanon

Lebanon continues to struggle with spillover from the Syrian conflict, including periodic sectarian violence; terrorist attacks; and the economic, political, and sectarian strain associated with refugees.

- Lebanon faces growing threats from terrorist groups, including the al-Nusrah Front and ISIL. Sunni extremists are trying to establish networks in Lebanon and have increased attacks against Lebanese army and Hizballah positions along the Lebanese-Syrian border. Lebanon potentially faces a protracted conflict in northern and eastern parts of the country from extremist groups seeking to seize Lebanese territory, supplies, and hostages.

- The presence of over one million mostly Sunni Syrian refugees in Lebanon, which has a population of only 4.1 million, has significantly altered Lebanon's sectarian demographics and is a continuing burden on the Lebanese economy. In October 2014, the cabinet further tightened entry restrictions to allow only "extreme humanitarian cases" into the country. Arrivals have declined 75 to 90 percent since August, most recently due in part to the new restrictions.

Egypt

Egyptian officials have announced that legislative elections will start in March 2015 and that voting will be staggered in phases over seven weeks. Egypt faces a persistent threat of terrorist and militant violence that is directed primarily at the state security forces both in the Sinai Peninsula and mainland Egypt. Since mid-2013, Sinai-based terrorist group Ansar Bayt al-Maqdis (ABM)—affiliated since November with ISIL—has claimed responsibility for some of the most sophisticated and deadly attacks against Egyptian security forces in decades.

Tunisia

Tunisia has transitioned to a permanent democratic government. Beji Caid Essebsi was elected President in the presidential runoff election in December 2014. In January 2015, Essebsi's political party Nidaa Tounes selected former Interior Minister Essid to become Prime Minister.

- In early February, Prime Minister Habib Essid formed a broad-based coalition government, led by Nidaa Tounes, which included Islamist party al-Nahda and several smaller parties. The new government almost certainly recognizes Tunisia's economic and security challenges.

The permanent government will inherit one of the highest youth unemployment rates in the world, a high budget deficit, and decreasing Foreign Direct Investment and balance of payments. It will struggle to meet public expectations for swift economic progress.

EUROPE

Turkey

Turkey will remain a critical partner in a wide range of US security policy priorities, including anti-ISIL and broader counterterrorism efforts. Joint US-Turkish efforts to stem instability in Iraq and Syria share the same goals but employ different approaches, increasing tension in the bilateral relationship. Turkish President Erdogan and leaders of the ruling Justice and Development Party (AKP) are focused on the general elections, which are scheduled to be held in June 2015

- Ankara will be more inclined to support the anti-ISIL coalition if the coalition agrees to focus efforts against Asad, including setting up an internationally guaranteed buffer zone in Syria.

- Turkey is concerned that the Kurdish Democratic Union (PYD)—a group it believes is affiliated with the Kurdistan People's Congress (KGK/former PKK)—will gain international legitimacy.

Key Partners

The Transatlantic partnership remains vital as the United States works with European leaders to maintain a concerted response to Russia's action in Ukraine and to other security challenges on the European continent and beyond. Europeans are working to address fiscal challenges and encourage economic growth while maintaining and strengthening financial governance.

- The Transatlantic Trade and Investment Partnership has the potential to help generate economic growth for both the United States and Europe, reinforce the transatlantic link, and address public concerns about data privacy and food and health standards.

RUSSIA AND EURASIA

Russia

The Ukrainian crisis has profoundly affected Russia's relations with the West and will have far-reaching effects on Russia's domestic politics, economic development, and foreign policy.

President Vladimir Putin enjoys some of his highest domestic approval ratings in all his years in office. An intense state media propaganda campaign has stoked Russians' perception that Putin righted a historical wrong in orchestrating Russia's seizure of Crimea and reasserted Russia's great-power interests against a hostile West.

At the same time, the crisis in Ukraine has exacerbated preexisting domestic problems in Russia. The fall of former Ukrainian President Viktor Yanukovych's government in February 2014 has almost certainly deepened the Kremlin's concerns over the dangers of mass demonstrations and has intensified the Kremlin's efforts to defuse what it sees as potential catalysts for protests in Russia.

Russia's economy was in decline even before the crisis began. Growth stagnated in 2014 due to declining oil prices, large capital outflows, and a sharply declining ruble. In addition, economic sanctions cut off some Russian firms from Western financing. These factors have increased the real and perceived risks of doing business in Russia, raised the overall cost of international credit, and will probably drive Russia into recession in 2015.

Moscow is pushing for greater regional integration, pressing neighboring states to follow the example of Belarus and Kazakhstan and join the Moscow-led Eurasian Economic Union. The Kremlin is also cultivating its relationship with China, seeking to maintain some influence in Europe and emphasizing multilateral forums to counter what Moscow views as US unilateralism. These trends were already present in Russian diplomacy, but the Ukrainian crisis has almost certainly lent emphasis to these policies.

Russia is taking information warfare to a new level, working to fan anti-US and anti-Western sentiment both within Russia and globally. Russian state-controlled media publish false and misleading information in an effort to discredit the West, undercut consensus on Russia, and build sympathy for Russian positions.

In Ukraine, Russia has demonstrated its willingness to covertly use military and paramilitary forces in a neighboring state—a development that raises anxieties in states along Russia's periphery. Future Russian deployments and force posture changes will probably be designed to maximize their diplomatic and public impact in Europe. Russian military officials have announced plans to conduct more "out-of-area" air and naval deployments, to include greater activity in the Caribbean and Mediterranean Seas.

Moscow has made headway in modernizing its nuclear and conventional forces, improving its training and joint operational proficiency, modernizing its military doctrine to integrate new methods of warfare, and developing long-range, precision-strike capabilities. Despite its economic difficulties, Moscow is committed to modernizing its military.

Ukraine, Moldova, and Belarus

Ukraine faces a daunting array of problems after nearly a year of conflict with Russia and its proxies in eastern Ukraine. At the same time, the crisis has fostered a sense of national identity and unity. Public opinion has shifted heavily in favor of pursuing integration with the EU while views of Russia have become sharply negative. Moreover, for the first time, a narrow majority of the population supports NATO membership.

Negotiations over the status of the separatist-held territory in eastern Ukraine will almost certainly be difficult and protracted. Russia has supplied substantial quantities of heavy weapons to strengthen the separatists' forces and covertly supports them with its own troops, both within Ukraine and from across the border. More importantly, Moscow has demonstrated that it is willing to intervene directly to prevent the separatists from being defeated on the battlefield. Further fighting is likely in 2015.

Ukraine's dire economic situation presents no less a challenge to Kyiv than the conflict in the east. Ukraine will be highly dependent on substantial outside financial assistance for years to come.

In Moldova, the narrow victory of pro-EU parties in the latest parliamentary elections suggests that Moldova will push ahead with its European integration agenda. However, Chisinau still faces numerous challenges in seeking to overcome economic difficulties, entrenched corruption, and Moscow's displeasure with Moldova's rejection of closer integration with Russia. Any progress on resolving the political status of the ethnic-Russian separatist region of Transnistria is unlikely.

On 1 January 2015, Belarus became, along with Kazakhstan, a founding member of the Eurasian Economic Union (EEU), a regional integration project that Moscow eventually plans to transform into a Eurasian Union as a counterpart to the EU. President Lukashenko has tread carefully in regard to the

Ukrainian crisis, declining to recognize Russia's seizure of Crimea, but agreeing nevertheless to deepen military cooperation with Moscow.

The Caucasus and Central Asia

In Georgia, progress is unlikely on the core disputes between Tbilisi and Moscow, including Georgia's NATO aspirations and the status of the occupied territories of Abkhazia and South Ossetia. Tensions with Russia will remain high, and we assess that Moscow will press Tbilisi to abandon closer EU and NATO ties.

Armenia and Azerbaijan saw an increase in 2014 of ceasefire violations and a record number of casualties along the Line of Contact (LOC), which separates ethnic Armenian and Azerbaijani forces near the separatist region of Nagorno-Karabakh. The increased violence highlights how the close proximity of opposing military forces continues to pose a risk of miscalculation and unintended escalation. Prospects for a peaceful resolution in the foreseeable future are dim.

Central Asian states remain concerned about regional instability in light of a reduced Coalition presence in Afghanistan. Although they have long been alarmed about the activities of Central Asian militant groups operating in Afghanistan and Pakistan, they are increasingly worried about the threat posed by the return of the small but growing number of their nationals who have traveled to Syria to join violent Islamist extremist groups. On the whole, however, the Central Asian states will probably face more acute risks of instability in 2015 from internal issues such as unclear political succession plans, weak economies, ethnic tensions, and political repression—any of which could produce a crisis with little warning.

EAST ASIA

China

China will continue to pursue an active foreign policy—especially within the Asia Pacific—bolstered by increasing capabilities and its firm stance on East and South China Sea territorial disputes with rival claimants. The chances for sustained tensions will persist because competing claimants will probably pursue actions—including energy exploration—that others perceive as infringing on their sovereignty. China will probably seek to expand its economic role and outreach in the region, pursuing broader acceptance of its economic initiatives, including the Asia Infrastructure Investment Bank. Although China remains focused on regional issues, it will seek a greater voice on major international issues and in making new international rules.

Notwithstanding this external agenda, Chinese leaders will focus primarily on addressing domestic concerns. The Chinese Communist Party leadership under President Xi Jinping announced an ambitious agenda of legal reforms in late 2014 that built on its previous agenda of ambitious economic reforms—all aimed at improving government efficiency and accountability and strengthening the control of the Communist Party. The difficulty of implementing these reforms and bureaucratic resistance to them create the possibility of rising internal frictions as the agenda moves forward. Beijing will also remain concerned about the potential for domestic unrest or terrorist acts in Xinjiang and Tibet, which might lead to renewed human rights abuses. Following months of pro-democracy protests in late 2014, Chinese leaders will monitor closely political developments in Hong Kong for signs of instability

North Korea

Three years after taking the helm of North Korea, Kim Jong Un has further solidified his position as unitary leader and final decision authority through purges, executions, and leadership shuffles. Kim was absent from public view for 40 days in late 2014, leading to widespread foreign media speculation about his health and the regime's stability. The focus on Kim's health s a reminder that the regime's stability might hinge on Kim's personal status. Kim has no clearly identified successor and is inclined to prevent the emergence of a clear "number two" who could consolidate power in his absence. Kim and the regime have publicly emphasized his focus on improving the country's troubled economy and the livelihood of the North Korean people while maintaining the tenets of a command economy. He has codified this approach via his dual-track policy of economic development and advancement of nuclear weapons. (Information on North Korea's nuclear weapons program and intentions can be found above in the section on WMD and Proliferation.) Despite renewed efforts at diplomatic outreach, Kim continues to challenge the international community with provocative and threatening behavior in pursuit of his goals, as prominently demonstrated in the November 2014 cyber attack on Sony.

SOUTH ASIA

Afghanistan

President Ashraf Ghani and Chief Executive Officer Abdullah Abdullah secured Parliament's approval of the Bilateral Security Agreement and NATO Status of Forces Agreement prior to the NATO Ministerial in December 2014. Despite the 12 January announcement of the r cabinet nominees, Ghani and Abdullah have yet to win legislative approval for all of those nominated or resolve the final details of their shared political powers derived from their national unity government agreement. Resolving these issues will require continued international engagement and support.

International financial aid remains the most important external determinant of the Kabul government's strength. However, the slow economic recovery from the global financial crisis has created fiscal challenges for many of Afghanistan's primary donors, particularly in Europe and Japan. These economic hurdles at home have reduced donors' enthusiasm and capacity to provide Afghanistan additional long-term financial aid above levels pledged through 2017 and reaffirmed in 2014 at the London Conference and NATO Wales Summit.

The Afghan National Security Forces (ANSF) prevented the Taliban from achieving a decisive military advantage in 2014. The ANSF, however, will require continued international security sector support and funding to stave off an increasingly aggressive Taliban insurgency through 2015. The ANSF, with the help of anti-Taliban powerbrokers and international funding, will probably maintain control of most major population centers. However, the forces will most likely cede control of some rural areas. Without international funding, the ANSF will probably not remain a cohesive or viable force.

The Taliban will probably remain largely cohesive under the leadership of Mullah Omar and sustain its countrywide campaign to take territory in outlying areas and steadily reassert influence over significant portions of the Pashtun countryside, positioning itself for greater territorial gains in 2015. Reliant on Afghanistan's opiate trade as a key domestic source of funding the Taliban will be able to exploit increasing opium poppy cultivation and potential heroin production for ready revenue. The Taliban has publicly touted the end of the mission of the International Security and Assistance Force (ISAF) and coalition drawdown as a sign of its inevitable victory, reinforcing its commitment to returning to power.

Pakistan

Pakistan will probably continue to implement some economic reforms and target anti-Pakistan militants and their activities.

* Prime Minister Sharif's promises to address economic, energy, and security issues almost certainly fell short of high public expectations. Furthermore, his standing weakened when he reportedly asked the Army to step in and handle opposition protests in late 2014.

* We assess that Islamabad will approve some additional economic reforms in 2015. Undertaking future economic and energy reforms will be more challenging and will probably face greater political and popular opposition.

* The Pakistan Government will probably focus in 2015 on diminishing the capabilities of the Tehrik-i-Taliban (TTP), which claimed the attack on a school in December—leaving over 100 children dead.

We judge that Pakistan will aim to establish positive rapport with the new Afghan Government, but longstanding distrust and unresolved disputes between the countries will prevent substantial progress.

* Pakistan's provision of safe haven to Lashkar-e Tayyiba will probably continue to be a key irritant in relations with India.

India

Prime Minister Narendra Modi's decisive leadership style, combined with the 2014 election of an absolute majority in the lower house of Parliament of his Bharatiya Janata Party (BJP), will enable more decisive Indian decisionmaking on domestic and foreign policy. Although India has a long-standing position that it maintain an independent policy, Modi will probably seek to work more closely with the United States on security, terrorism, and economic issues.

India wants to maintain a stable peace with Pakistan but views Pakistan as a direct terrorism threat and a regional source of instability.

India is concerned about the stability of Afghanistan and its own presence there following the drawdown of international forces and is looking for options to blunt the influence of Pakistani-supported groups and ensure that Afghanistan does not revert to a haven for anti-Indian militants.

Indian leaders will almost certainly pursue stronger economic ties with China that support the government's economic agenda of closing the trade gap and attracting investment in infrastructure. New Delhi's concern over perceived Chinese aggressiveness along the disputed border and in the Indian Ocean is probably growing in light of border incidents and the visit of a Chinese submarine to Sri Lanka in 2014.

SUB-SAHARAN AFRICA

Sub-Saharan Africa will face political and security challenges in 2015 including numerous presidential elections, ongoing insurgencies, and continuing intrastate conflict. The ongoing Ebola virus epidemic will undoubtedly challenge both Western African nations and the larger international community in trying to contain the virus' spread and counter economic degradation in fragile West African nations. Stability in South Sudan, Nigeria, Somalia, and the Central African Republic (CAR) will almost certainly remain tenuous throughout 2015.

West Africa

The Ebola virus will persist throughout West Africa in 2015, posing a significant threat to the economic viability and consequently the stability of the region. The continued drain on resources and unprecedented need for medical personnel will strain governments and economies in Liberia, Sierra Leone, and Guinea—the three worst-affected countries. Sustained financial and material assistance from the international community, continued domestic support for the governments' anti-Ebola efforts, and community engagement to change local misperceptions about the disease's cause, treatment options, and burial practices will remain critical to slowing the epidemic. Economic growth in the outbreak zone has already slowed and will continue to slow during 2015, straining budgets and probably increasing dependence on international donor aid. A prolonged or severe outbreak that continues well into 2015 might prompt Guinea to delay Presidential elections, increasing the possibility of election-related violence. Military and security services in the key outbreak countries will probably successfully contain isolated unrest and local hostility toward Ebola-response personnel.

Sudan

Khartoum will almost certainly confront a range of challenges, including continued insurgencies in the periphery, public dissatisfaction over continued economic decline, and potential protests surrounding its April 2015 elections. Sudanese economic conditions since South Sudan's independence in 2011 continue to deteriorate. Such conditions, including rising prices on staple goods, fuel opposition to the Sudanese Government.

South Sudan

Clashes between opposition forces and the Sudan People's Liberation Army (SPLA) will almost certainly increase during the dry season—which lasts from November to April—undermining ongoing peace talks and putting tenuous humanitarian gains at risk. Peace talks between Juba and opposition elements will probably remain slow-going.

Nigeria

Instability in Nigeria will probably increase in 2015, given contentious elections delayed until March and April, plummeting oil revenue, and the military's inability to check Boko Haram's ascendancy in the northeast. The election will occasion violence, with prospects for protests in the months following the election. In addition, militants might remobilize in the Niger Delta and attack the oil industry. Boko Haram will probably continue to solidify control over its self-declared Islamic state in northeastern Nigeria and expand its terror campaign in neighboring Nigerian states, Cameroon, Niger, and Chad. Abuja's reliance on oil exports for revenue will almost certainly ensure that Nigeria remains vulnerable to fluctuations in the global oil market in 2015. Declining oil prices will probably squeeze government revenues and drain currency reserves. Abuja's overtaxed security forces will have a limited ability to anticipate and preempt threats.

Somalia

In Somalia, al-Shabaab is conducting asymmetric attacks against government facilities and Western targets in and around Mogadishu. The credibility and effectiveness of the young Somali Government will be further threatened by persistent political infighting; ill-equipped government institutions; and pervasive technical, political, and administrative shortfalls.

Lord's Resistance Army

The Lord's Resistance Army (LRA), even in its weakened state, probably has the ability to regenerate if counter-LRA operations are reduced. The LRA continues to display great agility in its geographic areas of operation and in the operational security of its activities.

Central African Republic

Despite the presence of international peacekeeping forces, the risk of continued ethno-religious clashes between Christians and Muslims throughout the country, including in the capital, remains high.

The Sahel

Governments in Africa's Sahel region—particularly Chad, Niger, Mali, and Mauritania—will remain at risk of terrorist attacks and possible internal conflict. Al-Qa'ida in the Lands of the Islamic Maghreb (AQIM) and affiliated groups are committed to continuing their terrorist activity in the Sahel, including against Western interests. They will probably seek to increase the frequency and scale of attacks in northern Mali. Sahelien militaries will struggle to handle a wide array of security threats.

LATIN AMERICA AND THE CARIBBEAN

Cuba

Cuban President Raul Castro's focus will almost certainly be preparing the country for the eventual end of the Castro era and maintaining tight political control. He is cautiously implementing economic and leadership reforms and released dozens of political prisoners in early January. Cuba's principal interest in normalizing relations with the United States is probably linked to its recognition of the need to ease discontent over dismal living conditions and poor economic prospects. The slow rollout of economic reforms and a fall in nickel output cut GDP growth to 1.2 percent in 2014. Crucial components of the economic reform program—reducing the state role in the economy and opening up a few opportunities for self-employment—will probably produce numerous, short-term economic dislocations before gradually increasing productivity and jobs.

Cuba's population of 11 million has been declining since about 2005 because of falling birthrates and emigration. Cuban migrant arrivals at the US southwest border rose from 10,400 in FY12 to 17,300 in FY14. Maritime arrivals and interdictions will probably increase in 2015 because of rumors that if the two countries normalize relations, the United States would change immigration policies that allow Cubans who reach the United States to obtain status.

Central America

Weak institutions, poor economic prospects, and the growing strength of criminal gangs will probably limit the ability of the governments of Central America's northern tier—El Salvador, Guatemala, and Honduras—to improve rule of law, job opportunities, and citizen security, which will probably continue to fuel immigration to the United States in 2015. Fractured legislatures, political challenges, and entrenched business interests will probably slow agreement on raising some of the lowest tax collection rates in the world or adopting economic and social policies that would help reduce the high rates of poverty that spur migration to the United States. About 25 percent of **El Salvador's** population has emigrated during the past two decades, mostly to the United States, because of lack of economic opportunities and widespread insecurity. El Salvador's economy has experienced the lowest economic growth rates in the region for eight consecutive years. **Guatemala's** weak fiscal position will undermine efforts to ameliorate extreme poverty, particularly in rural areas. About 1.6 million Guatemalans reside in the United States and send about $5.5 billion in remittances back home each year. **Honduras,** one of the hemisphere's poorest countries, is struggling to make headway against ineffective, corrupt institutions. Honduras has the world's highest rate of homicides per capita, despite a reported modest decline in 2014, and criminal gangs are forcibly recruiting youth and extorting businesses and individuals.

Venezuela

Like most oil-exporting nations, Venezuela is experiencing the economic consequences of policy choices and the decline in global oil prices. Oil accounts for about 95 percent of Venezuelan export earnings and 45 percent of government revenue. Caracas will face a strained fiscal environment in 2015 along with rising inflation and shortages of essential goods.

Legislative elections are slated to occur by the end of 2015; voters will be concerned about public security, the economy, and political rights. President Nicolas Maduro appointed a presidential commission to review the country's police system and recommend reforms after the high-profile murder of a national assembly deputy and a violent law enforcement confrontation in October 2014 with a radical, armed group known as a *colectivo.*

Haiti

Political tensions between Haitian President Martelly and his opponents will probably flare during 2015 and might undermine preparations for overdue local and parliamentary elections as well as for the vote for a new president in November 2015. Haiti will need substantial technical and financial support from the international community to organize and hold elections. Some violent protests are probable and might become more intense or widespread if political opponents believe that electoral preparations favor Martelly's party or allies.

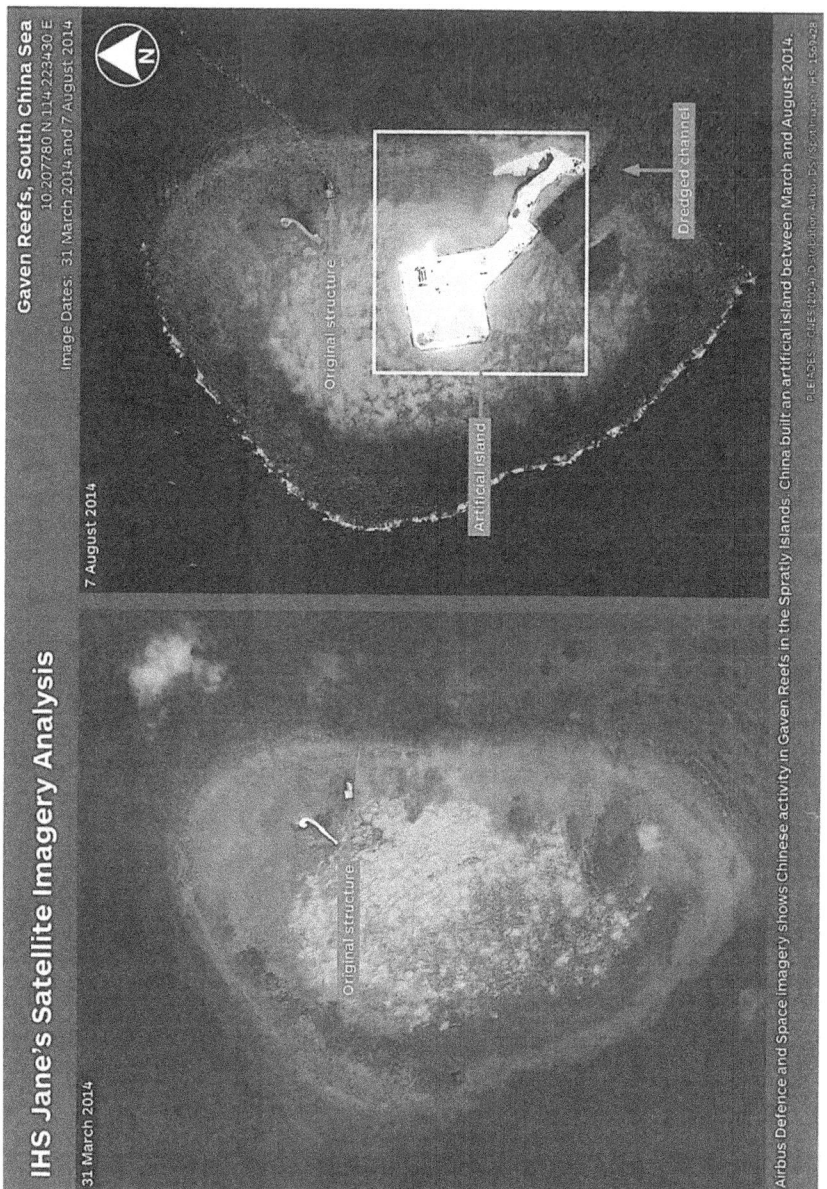

STATEMENT OF LT. GEN. VINCENT STEWART, DIRECTOR OF THE DEFENSE INTELLIGENCE AGENCY

General STEWART. Mr. Chairman, in the interest of time, we have the statement for the record and just one oral statement from Director Clapper.

[The prepared statement of General Stewart follows:]

Statement for the Record

Worldwide Threat Assessment

Armed Services Committee

United States Senate

Vincent R. Stewart, Lieutenant General, U.S. Marine Corps

Director, Defense Intelligence Agency

Information available as of February 20, 2015 was used in the preparation of this assessment

Table of Contents Page

INTRODUCTION
Iraq and Afghanistan ... 4
Terrorism ... 7
    Al-Qa'ida in the Arabian Peninsula (AQAP) ... 8
    Al-Qa'ida in Lands of the Islamic Maghreb (AQIM) ... 8
    Al-Nusrah Front
    Khorasan Group ... 8
    Islamic Revolutionary Guard Corps-Qods Force (IRGC-QF) ... 8
    Boko Haram ... 9

REGIONAL THREATS
Russia ... 9
East Asia
    China ... 10
    North Korea ... 12
Middle East and North Africa
    Iran ... 13
    Syria ... 14
    Libya ... 15
    Egypt ... 15
    Yemen ... 15
South Asia
    Pakistan ... 16
    India ... 16
Africa
    Somalia ... 17
    Nigeria ... 17
Latin America
    Mexico ... 18
    Colombia ... 18
    Venezuela ... 18
    Honduras, El Salvador, and Guatemala ... 19

GLOBAL THREATS
U.S. Space Systems and Services ... 19
Cyber ... 20
Proliferation of WMD and Ballistic Missiles ... 21
Proliferation of Advanced Conventional Weapons ... 21
Infectious Diseases ... 22
Foreign Intelligence & Insider Threats ... 22

INTRODUCTION

Chairman McCain, Ranking Member Reed, and Members of the Committee, thank you for the invitation to provide the Defense Intelligence Agency's (DIA) assessment of the global security environment and to address the threats facing the nation. A confluence of global political, military, social, and technological developments, taken in aggregate, have created security challenges more diverse and complex than those we have experienced in our lifetimes.

Our challenges range from highly capable, near-peer competitors to empowered individuals and the concomitant reduction in our own capacity will make those challenges all the more stressing on our defense and intelligence establishments. This strategic environment will be with us for some time, and the threat's increasing scope, volatility, and complexity will be the "new normal."

The 16,500 men and women of DIA stationed around the globe are confronting this rapidly evolving defense landscape head-on, and leading the Intelligence Community (IC) in providing unique defense intelligence from the strategic to the tactical level to deliver a decision advantage to warfighters, defense planners, the defense acquisition community, and policymakers. The men and women – both uniformed and civilian – of your DIA know they have a vital responsibility to the American people and take great pride in their work. I am privileged to serve with them and present their analysis to you. My hope is that this hearing will help the nation – through the important oversight role of Congress – to better understand the diversity of the global challenges we face and to support this committee in developing possible responses to these threats. Thank you for your confidence and support.

I will begin first with an assessment of Iraq, followed by Afghanistan, where the Department of Defense (DoD), DIA, the IC, and our Coalition partners are on the front lines, actively supporting military operations against threats from the Islamic State of Iraq and the Levant (ISIL), al-Qa'ida, and the Taliban. I will then transition to a selected group of violent extremist organizations, and conclude with other regional challenges and global threats.

IRAQ AND AFGHANISTAN

ISIL's resurgence since the withdrawal of U.S. forces from Iraq in 2011 was vividly displayed by the group's rapid advance across much of northern and western Iraq last spring. Since that time, Coalition airstrikes have removed a number of ISIL senior leaders and degraded the group's ability to operate openly in Iraq and Syria. We expect ISIL to continue entrenching itself and consolidating gains in Sunni areas of Iraq and Syria while also fighting for territory outside those areas. We also expect ISIL to continue limited offensive operations, such as the group's recent operations in Syria and Anbar province of Iraq. Seizing and holding Shia and Kurdish-populated areas of Iraq have been, and will continue to be difficult for ISIL in 2015. ISIL's ability to govern the areas it has captured in Iraq and Syria, and its ability to keep the support – or at least acquiescence – of the Sunni population will be key indicators of the success or failure of the self-declared "Islamic state." With affiliates in Algeria, Egypt, and Libya, the group is beginning to assemble a growing international footprint that includes ungoverned and under-governed areas. Similarly, the flow of foreign fighters into, and out of, Syria and Iraq – many of whom are aligned with ISIL– is troubling.

Defeats of Iraqi Security Forces (ISF) and the collapse of multiple army divisions highlight large-scale institutional deficiencies within the ISF. Several of the more concerning deficiencies include poor logistics and endemic corruption that has bred ineffective commanders and led to poor morale. Force generation efforts will be complicated by a lack of experienced and qualified soldiers. Local and tribal pro-government forces suffer from similar supply and manning shortages.

The ISF remains unable to defend against external threats or sustain conventional military operations against internal challenges without foreign assistance. Iraq is diversifying its defense acquisitions through numerous foreign military sales including with Russia and other non-U.S. suppliers to overcome equipment shortfalls and capability gaps. These decisions are reducing ISF interoperability.

Turning to Afghanistan, the still-developing Afghan National Security Forces (ANSF) remain stalemated with the Taliban-led insurgency. In 2015, we expect the ANSF to maintain stability and security in Kabul and key urban areas while retaining freedom of movement on major highways. However, the Taliban, al-Qa'ida, and their extremist allies will likely seek to exploit the reduced Coalition presence by pressuring ANSF units in rural areas, conducting high profile attacks in major population centers, and expanding their safe havens.

ANSF will remain reliant on Coalition enablers for air, intelligence, and maintenance support. As NATO and our allies carry out their scheduled drawdown, the ANSF will struggle to effectively replace these lost enablers, deal with interoperability challenges between the army and police, and address persistent maintenance and logistical issues.

The Afghan National Army (ANA) is the most proficient security institution in Afghanistan, and has shown the capacity to plan and conduct multi-corps operations in high-threat areas. However, the ANA will continue to struggle with permanently denying the insurgents freedom of movement in rural areas, and will remain constrained by its stretched airlift and logistical capacity. High attrition also continues to plague the force, which has struggled to keep its numbers near full capacity.

The Afghan National Police (ANP) provide sufficient presence and security within urban centers and provincial and district hubs, but remain vulnerable in controlling high-threat, rural areas. ANP challenges include manpower shortages, inadequate training, attrition, logistics shortfalls, and the corrosive influence of corruption. These factors have diminished the effectiveness of the ANP and undermined its popular image.

In 2014, the Afghan Air Force (AAF) improved its support to ground operations, significantly increasing the number of casualty evacuation missions and forward deployments of Mi-17 transport helicopters and Mi-35 gunships into contested areas. Despite these improvements, the AAF is not a reliable source of close air support and still struggles with recruiting qualified pilots and technicians.

The development of ANSF capabilities in 2015 will be critical as the insurgency will again attempt to increase its influence in rural areas, operate in larger formations, and continue to test security forces by temporarily seizing a number of vulnerable rural Afghan checkpoints and district centers. This will include increased high profile attacks, particularly in Kabul, where the Taliban seeks to undermine perceptions of Afghan security. The Taliban will probably sustain the capability to propagate a rural-based insurgency that can project intermittent attacks in urban areas through at least 2018.

TERRORISM

Al-Qa'ida core is now focused on physical survival following battlefield losses. At the same time, the group is trying to retain its status as the vanguard of the global extremist movement, being eclipsed now by ISIL's rising global prominence and powerful competition for adherents. Al-Qa'ida core in Pakistan continues to retain the loyalty of its global affiliates in Yemen, Somalia, North Africa, Syria, and South Asia.

Despite ongoing counterterrorism (CT) pressure and competition from ISIL, al-Qa'ida will likely retain a transnational attack capability, and will likely try to expand its limited presence in eastern Afghanistan as Western CT operations there decline. Beyond core al-Qa'ida, I would like to highlight for the committee a handful of other violent extremist groups that are of particular concern to DIA.

Al-Qa'ida in the Arabian Peninsula (AQAP) remains committed to attacking the West, probably by targeting commercial aviation with innovative explosives, and will leverage instability in Yemen to its advantage.

Al-Qa'ida in Lands of the Islamic Maghreb (AQIM) recently increased efforts to expand its operating areas across North and West Africa by working with, and through, other regional terrorist groups. AQIM almost certainly continues to plan attacks and kidnapping operations against U.S. allies in the region.

As part of the larger al-Qa'ida network, we are concerned about the support **al-Nusrah Front** provides to transnational terrorist attack plotting against U.S. and Western interests.

The **Khorasan Group** is a cadre of experienced al-Qa'ida operatives that works closely with al-Nusrah Front. Although coalition airstrikes have killed a number of senior Khorasan Group members, the group almost certainly will maintain the intent to continue plotting against Western interests unless completely destroyed.

Islamic Revolutionary Guard Corps-Qods Force (IRGC-QF) and Lebanese Hizballah are instruments of Iran's foreign policy and its ability to project power in Iraq, Syria, and beyond. Hizballah continues to support the Syrian regime, pro-regime militants and Iraqi Shia militants in Syria. Hizballah trainers and advisors in Iraq assist Iranian and Iraqi Shia militias fighting Sunni extremists there. Select Iraqi Shia militant groups also warned of their willingness to fight U.S. forces returning to Iraq.

Boko Haram's (BH) offensive in northeastern Nigeria, largely against the Nigerian government, includes near daily attacks. If continued, BH's successes could grow into a significant regional crisis with implications outside northwest Africa.

REGIONAL THREATS

RUSSIA

Russia has made significant progress modernizing its nuclear and conventional forces, improving its training and joint operational proficiency, modernizing its military doctrine to integrate new methods of warfare, and developing long range precision strike capabilities. Despite its economic difficulties, Moscow is fully committed to modernizing both nuclear and conventional forces. At the same time, Russian forces have conducted exercises and a record number of out-of-area air and naval operations. We expect these to continue this year to include greater activity in the Caribbean and Mediterranean Seas.

In 2014, Moscow moved to shape events in Ukraine, employing its improved military capabilities to create a long-term conflict in Ukraine's Donetsk and Luhansk regions. All indications are that Moscow will continue to employ a mix of military and nonmilitary pressure against Kyiv this year, to include the use of propaganda and information operations, cyberspace operations, covert agents, regular military personnel operating as "volunteers," mercenaries, arms transfers to the separatists, and the threat of military intervention. These actions are consistent with Russia's new military doctrine

Moscow affirmed its intent to improve the military's capability to control the Russian Arctic region, stressing the area's current and future strategic and economic importance.

In December Moscow announced the activation of a Joint Service Command (OSK) North, highlighting the importance of the Arctic to Russian leaders.

Russia will continue to place the highest priority on the maintenance of a robust and capable arsenal of strategic nuclear weapons. Priorities for the strategic nuclear forces include the modernization of its road-mobile intercontinental ballistic missiles (ICBMs) and upgrades to strategic forces' command and control facilities. In the next year, Russia will field more road-mobile SS-27 Mod-2 ICBMs with multiple independently targetable re-entry vehicles. It also will continue development of the RS-26 ballistic missile, the Dolgorukiy ballistic missile submarine, its SS-N-32 Bulava submarine-launched ballistic missile, and next-generation air- and ground-launched cruise missiles.

EAST ASIA

China's People's Liberation Army (PLA) is building a modern military capable of defending China's "core interests" of preserving its political system, protecting territorial integrity and sovereignty (China views these to include Taiwan and other contested claims to land and water), and ensuring sustainable economic and social development.

The PLA remains focused on transforming the army into a fully mechanized force. The PLA is converting its divisions into brigades to increase lethality and improve combat capabilities. China's national-level training focus has been on brigade-level exercises that stress unit combat mission capabilities under realistic conditions, long distance mobility, and command and control. We expect these trends to continue.

The PLA Navy continues to expand its operational and deployment areas. China's first aircraft carrier, commissioned in late 2012, will not reach its full potential until it acquires a fully operational fixed-wing air regiment, but we expect the navy will make progress toward its goal this year.

The South China Sea (SCS) remains a potential flashpoint. Overlapping claims among China, Vietnam, the Philippines, Malaysia, Taiwan, and Brunei– exacerbated by large-scale construction or major steps to militarize or expand law enforcement– has increased tensions among claimants. This has prompted an increase in defense acquisition, to include submarine capabilities, in some of these countries.

In 2014, China twice deployed submarines to the Indian Ocean. The submarines probably conducted area familiarization to form a baseline for increasing China's power projection. China continues production of JIN-class nuclear-powered ballistic missile submarines and submarine-launched ballistic missiles. We expect China to conduct its first nuclear deterrence patrols this year.

The PLA Air Force (PLAAF) is approaching modernization on a scale unprecedented in its history. China now has two stealth fighter programs - the third and fourth J-20 prototypes, which conducted their first flights in March and July 2014. Further PLAAF developments are anticipated.

China's nuclear arsenal currently consists of 50-60 ICBMs. China is adding more survivable road-mobile systems, enhancing its silo-based systems, and developing a sea-based nuclear deterrent. They are also augmenting more than 1,200 conventional short-range ballistic missiles deployed opposite Taiwan with a limited but growing number of conventionally armed, medium-range ballistic missiles, including the DF-16, which will improve China's ability to strike regional targets. China continues to deploy growing numbers of the DF-21D antiship ballistic missile and is developing a tiered ballistic missile defense system, having successfully tested the upper-tier capability on two occasions.

The **Democratic People's Republic of Korea's (DPRK)** primary goals are preserving the control of the Kim family regime, improving its poor economy, and deterring attack by improving its strategic and conventional military capabilities. Pyongyang maintains that nuclear and ballistic missile capabilities are essential to ensure its sovereignty.

The DPRK continues to prioritize maintaining the readiness of its large, forward-deployed forces. While Pyongyang is stressing increased realism in military training, exercises still appear to do little more than maintain basic competencies. Because of its conventional military deficiencies, the DPRK is also concentrating on improving its deterrence capabilities, especially its nuclear technology and ballistic missile forces.

We believe the DPRK continues to develop its nuclear weapons and missile programs which pose a serious threat to the U.S. and regional allies. We remain concerned that the DPRK will conduct a nuclear test in the future. Following the United Nations' (U.N.) condemnation of its human rights record in November 2014, Pyongyang indicated it would "not refrain any further from conducting a nuclear test." This followed a statement in March 2014 wherein North Korea's Foreign Ministry warned it "would not rule out a new form of nuclear test."

Pyongyang is also making efforts to expand and modernize its deployed close-, short-, medium-, and intermediate-range systems. It seeks to develop longer-range ballistic missiles capable of delivering nuclear weapons to the U.S., and continues efforts to bring its KN08 road-mobile ICBM to operational capacity. In 2015, North Korea will continue improving the combat proficiency of its deployed ballistic missile force, and will work to improve missile designs to boost overall capability. Pyongyang likely will launch additional ballistic missiles as part of its training and research and development process. We remain concerned by North Korea's illicit proliferation activities and attempts to evade U.N. sanctions.

MIDDLE EAST AND NORTH AFRICA

The Islamic Republic of Iran continues to threaten U.S. strategic interests in the Middle East. Iran's actions and policies are designed to further its goal of becoming the dominant regional power, as well as enhance its strategic depth.

Tehran views the U.S. as its most capable adversary and has fashioned its military strategy and doctrine accordingly. Iran's military posture is primarily defensive and is designed to deter an attack, survive an initial attack if deterrence fails, and retaliate against its aggressor to force a diplomatic resolution. Iran's numerous underground facilities have helped reduce its military vulnerabilities. We do not anticipate any changes to this posture in 2015.

We continue to assess Iran's goal is to develop capabilities that will allow it to build missile-deliverable nuclear weapons, should a decision be made to do so. The regime faces no insurmountable technical barriers to producing a nuclear weapon, making Iran's political will the central issue.

Iran's overall defense strategy relies on a substantial inventory of theater ballistic missiles capable of reaching as far as southeastern Europe. Iran continues to develop more sophisticated missiles, and is improving the range and accuracy of its current missile systems. Iran publicly stated that it intends to launch a space-launch vehicle as early as this year capable of ICBM ranges, if configured as such.

Iran is also steadily improving its military capabilities. The navy is developing faster, more lethal surface vessels, growing its submarine force, expanding its cruise missile defense capabilities, and increasing its presence in international waters. The navy aspires to travel as far as the Atlantic Ocean.

Iran is laboring to modernize its air and air defense forces under the weight of international sanctions. Each year, Iran unveils what it claims are state-of-the-art, Iranian-made systems, including surface-to-air missiles (SAMs), radars, and unmanned aerial vehicles. It continues to seek an advanced long-range SAM.

We assess the conflict in **Syria** is trending in the Asad regime's favor, which holds the military advantage in Aleppo - Syria's largest city. In 2015, we anticipate the regime's strategy will be to encircle Aleppo, cut opposition supply lines, and besiege the opposition. Hizballah and Iran, Damascus' key allies in its fight against the opposition, continue to provide training, advice, and extensive logistical support to the Syrian government and its supporters. Despite the regime's military advantage – particularly in firepower and air superiority – it will continue to struggle and be unable to decisively defeat the opposition in 2015.

In **Libya,** political instability and ongoing militia violence have worsened over the year, exacerbating conditions that have already made Libya an attractive terrorist safe haven. ISIL has increased its presence and influence in Libya, particularly in Darnah, where it has begun establishing Islamic institutions. Without a unified government and capable military, there is limited possibility of stability in the near-term.

As **Egypt** prepares for parliamentary elections this spring, its leaders are facing numerous security concerns driven by regional unrest and several major terrorist attacks in 2014. Egyptian security forces face frequent attacks in Sinai and the Nile Valley despite suppressing most of the political unrest last year. Egyptians have also been attacked from and within Libyan territory. Egypt has responded to these attacks by increasing its CT campaign in Sinai and tightening security on the Gaza and Libya borders to reduce militant and arms flow into Egypt. Egypt has also responded to attacks on its citizens in Libya with airstrikes and has called on the international coalition fighting ISIL to include Libya in the fight. The upcoming year will likely see Egyptian security forces stressed by internal terrorist activities and efforts to manage instability in Libya.

In **Yemen,** instability has increased since the Huthis, a northern Zaydi Shia group with Iranian ties, captured the Presidential Palace in mid-January and attained senior positions in nearly all key Yemeni government and security institutions. Current conditions are providing AQAP operational space. Meanwhile, Yemen's neighbors are increasingly concerned about instability spilling across their borders, potentially spreading another humanitarian crisis in the region.

SOUTH ASIA

Pakistan Army ground operations in North Waziristan Agency (NWA) have cleared antistate militants from most population centers, and we expect the military will continue targeting remaining militant strongholds in 2015. The December 2014 Tehrik-e Taliban Pakistan (TTP) Peshawar attack against the army-run school that killed more than 140 people, mostly children, spurred the government and military to implement a national action plan against terrorism, including the establishment of military courts.

Despite ongoing military operations, Pakistan will continue to face internal security threats from militant, sectarian, and separatist groups and remains concerned about ISIL outreach and propaganda in South Asia.

India is in the midst of a major military modernization effort to address problems with its aging equipment and to better posture itself to defend against both Pakistan and China. New Delhi is working to address impediments to modernization, such as its cumbersome procurement process, budget constraints, and an inefficient domestic defense industry. India's relationship with Pakistan remains strained, marked by periodic skirmishes on or near the Line of Control that separates Indian and Pakistani Kashmir, resulting in the highest number of civilian casualties since 2003. Occasional unofficial Track-II dialogue resulted in little progress in resolving bilateral disputes.

New Delhi and Beijing maintain limited military-to-military engagement and continue to discuss their longstanding border dispute, despite occasional altercations between troops patrolling the border. India's concern over increased Chinese activity in South Asia has pushed New Delhi to base advanced fighter aircraft and to raise additional ground forces opposite the China border.

India continues to conduct periodic tests of its nuclear-capable missiles to enhance and verify missile reliability and capabilities. India will continue developing an ICBM, the Agni-VI, which will reportedly carry multiple warheads, and is working on the development of several variants of a submarine-launched ballistic missile.

AFRICA

Security conditions in **Somalia** improved in 2014 as progress was made against al-Shabaab, but challenges remain. The African Union Mission in Somalia (AMISOM) and the Somali National Army (SNA) conducted two rounds of offensive operations, liberating several al-Shabaab-held towns in south-central Somalia, including the lucrative port city of Baraawe. Somali militia participated in these operations, but remains unable to maintain control of cleared areas due to a number of factors, including endemic corruption and underlying clan tensions. Mogadishu's focus on governance and force integration efforts should help decrease prospects for instability as regional administrations evolve during the next year.

Nigeria's presidential election, now scheduled for 28 March to allow for additional security measures, will probably be the closest and most contentious since civilian rule was restored in 1999. Violence throughout the election – and probably thereafter – will stretch security and military forces thin. The military leadership – often focused on advancing private gain over strategic imperatives – has failed to properly resource and train troops. Nigeria recently acquired new weapons systems, but troops lack the training and motivation to effectively employ them. This instability is likely to lead to massive population displacements, more civilian deaths and kidnappings, growing extremist safe havens, and refugee spillover into neighboring countries.

LATIN AMERICA

In Latin America, transnational threats such as drug- and arms- trafficking and special interest alien transit, coupled with porous borders, have increased insecurity and challenged stability and prosperity. Moreover, outside actors are increasingly seeking to challenge the U.S. as the defense partner of choice in the region.

Mexico remains the principal transit country for U.S.-bound cocaine, and the primary foreign supplier of methamphetamine, heroin, and marijuana to the U. S. Civilian and military security force pressure on all major drug trafficking groups has likely contributed to the decline in drug-related homicides.

The **Colombian** government has made significant progress reducing cocaine production. While no longer the top cocaine producer globally, it remains the principal supplier of cocaine to the U.S. Drug profits fund insurgent and illegal armed groups, which increasingly work directly with Mexican drug cartels.

Venezuelan President Nicolás Maduro has not resolved the factors that contributed to nationwide anti-government protests in 2014, including a poor economy, shortages of basic goods, unchecked violent crime, and the government's authoritarian tactics against the political opposition. We anticipate student organizations and the political opposition will stage protests in the months leading up to 2015 legislative elections. Military leaders have remained loyal and will continue to quell anti-government protests. We anticipate security forces occasionally will use heavy-handed tactics to restore order.

In **Honduras, El Salvador, and Guatemala**, violence levels tied to gang, drug, and criminal activity remain amongst the highest in the world.

GLOBAL THREATS

The threat to **U.S. space systems and services** will increase as potential adversaries pursue disruptive and destructive counterspace capabilities. Rapidly evolving commercial space technology will support the global pursuit of enhanced space and counterspace capabilities that may narrow the technological gap with the U.S.

Chinese and Russian military leaders understand the unique information advantages afforded by space systems and are developing capabilities to deny U.S. use of space in the event of a conflict. Chinese military writings specifically highlight the need to interfere with, damage, and destroy reconnaissance, navigation, and communication satellites. China has satellite jamming capabilities and is pursuing other antisatellite systems. In July 2014, China conducted a non-destructive antisatellite missile test. A previous destructive test with this same system in 2007 created long-lived space debris.

Russia's military doctrine emphasizes space defense as a vital component of its national defense. Russian leaders openly assert that the Russian armed forces have antisatellite weapons and conduct antisatellite research.

The global **cyber threat** environment presents numerous persistent challenges to the security and integrity of DoD networks and information. Threat actors now demonstrate an increased ability and willingness to conduct aggressive cyberspace operations—including both service disruptions and espionage—against U.S. and allied defense information networks. Similarly, we note with increasing concern recent destructive cyber actions against U.S. private-sector networks demonstrating capabilities that could hold U.S. government and defense networks at risk.

For 2015, we expect espionage against U.S. government defense and defense contractor networks to continue largely unabated, while destructive network attack capabilities continue to develop and proliferate worldwide. We are also concerned about the threat to the integrity of U.S. defense procurement networks posed by supply chain vulnerabilities from counterfeit and sub-quality components.

Threat actors increasingly are willing to incorporate cyber options into regional and global power projection capabilities. The absence of universally accepted and enforceable norms of behavior in cyberspace contributes to this situation. In response, states worldwide are forming "cyber command" organizations and developing national capabilities. Similarly, cyberspace operations are playing increasingly important roles in regional conflicts—for example, in eastern Ukraine—where online network disruptions, espionage, disinformation and propaganda activities are now integral to the conflict.

Iran and North Korea now consider disruptive and destructive cyberspace operations a valid instrument of statecraft, including during what the U.S. considers peacetime. These states likely view cyberspace operations as an effective means of imposing costs on their adversaries while limiting the likelihood of damaging reprisals.

Non-state actors often express the desire to conduct malicious cyber attacks, but likely lack the capability to conduct high-level cyber operations. However, non-state actors, such as Hizballah, AQAP, and ISIL will continue during the next year to effectively use the Internet for communication, propaganda, fundraising and recruitment.

The **proliferation and potential use of weapons of mass destruction (WMD) and ballistic missiles** is a grave and enduring threat. Securing nuclear weapons, materials, and the scientific capabilities to develop chemical and biological weapons is a worldwide imperative. The time when only a few states had access to the most dangerous technologies is past, and the use of chemicals in Syria further demonstrates the threat of WMD is real.
China will continue to be a source of dual-use WMD-applicable goods, equipment, and materials to countries of concern, like Iran, North Korea, and Syria. North Korea is among the world's leading suppliers of ballistic missiles and related technologies and, despite the adoption of U.N. Security Council resolutions, the DPRK continues proliferating weapons-related materiel. Russia, China, Iran, and North Korea engage in national-level military denial and deception programs that include the use of underground facilities to conceal and protect WMDs, and command, control, and other strategic assets and functions.

The **proliferation of advanced conventional weapons,** especially air defense systems and antiship cruise missiles, is a military issue of growing concern. Russian exports of these arms, including the SA-17, SA-22, SA-20 SAM systems and the SS-N-26 Yakhont supersonic antiship cruise missile is particularly troubling. Russia has exported several of these systems to countries of concern, including the SA-17 to Venezuela, and the SA-17, SA-22 and Yakhont to Syria. The 300-kilometer-range Yakhont poses a major threat to U.S. naval operations particularly in the eastern Mediterranean. There are no signs these sales will abate in 2015. If Russia was to sell the SA-20 to Iran, it would significantly increase Iranian military capabilities.

Infectious diseases are emerging as a global health concern. The Ebola epidemic in West Africa is the most visible reminder that health issues can suddenly materialize from anywhere and threaten American lives and interests. Our ability to mitigate and control health threats before they impact the U. S. relies on early warning, despite the absence of precise indicators of when and where new diseases will emerge. Pandemic warning likely will become more challenging and complex in 2015.

Finally, **foreign intelligence threats** from Russian, Chinese, and Cuban intelligence services continue to be a challenge. Trusted insiders who disclose sensitive U.S. information for nefarious purposes will also remain a significant threat in 2015. The technical sophistication of this insider threat exacerbates the challenge.

Chairman MCCAIN. Thank you.

Director Clapper, on the issue of defensive weaponry to Ukraine, do you believe that, if we give that assistance, that it would escalate—provoke Putin to escalate his assistance to the, quote, ''separatists'' and his aggression against Ukraine?

Mr. CLAPPER. Well, General Breedlove discussed this recently, and he did make, I think, a very apt comment, and, you know, predicting exactly what Putin will do or what his behavior will be is something of an unknown. I think the intelligence community view is that, if we were to provide lethal assistance to Ukraine, that this would evoke a negative reaction from Putin and the Russians. It could potentially further remove the very thin figleaf of their position that they're not—have not been involved in Ukraine, and could lead to accelerating or promoting more weaponry and higher sophistication into the separatist areas to support the separatists. But, I hasten to add, this is an intelligence community assessment, and this is not necessarily to suggest opposition to provision of lethal aid.

Chairman McCain. Well, I'm glad you added that, because my next question is, What more do you think that Putin would do—could do? Go to Kiev?

Mr. Clapper. Sir, we don't——

Chairman McCain. They certainly—the weaponry he's using now is his most sophisticated weaponry.

Mr. Clapper. We don't—well, he could bring in a lot more if he wanted to, and——

Chairman McCain. He could bring in more——

Mr. Clapper.—certainly more volumes of it.

Chairman McCain. To do what?

Mr. Clapper. Well, for example, armed helicopters——

Chairman McCain. Yeah, to do—to achieve what goal?

Mr. Clapper. Well, it is not our assessment that he is bent on capturing or conquering all of Ukraine. He certainly wants——

Chairman McCain. Absolutely.

Mr. Clapper.—I believe he wants a whole—from an infrastructure standpoint—entity, I believe, composed of the two oblasts in eastern Ukraine—

Chairman McCain. Which he's already——

Mr. Clapper.—to include, perhaps——

Chairman McCain:—achieving.

Mr. Clapper.—a land bridge to Crimea and perhaps a port—specifically, Mariupol. We do not believe that an attack on Mariupol is imminent. Think they're in the mode now of reconstituting and regrouping after the major confrontation in Debaltseve.

Chairman McCain. Well, I have to tell you that I disagree with you. They're already increasing activities around Mariupol, and I will predict to you now he will put additional pressure on Mariupol, because he wants to establish the land bridge there. Just as some of us predicted exactly what he's doing now.

And to say that we're worried about provoking him, he's not going to go to Kiev. He's going to establish the land bridge to Crimea, and then he's going to figure out whether he should go to Moldova, or not. He's already putting intense pressure on the Baltics. We all know that. We don't have to have intelligence reports to get that.

So, this idea that somehow we will provoke Vladimir Putin—he's done everything he wanted to do, General. You tell me what he didn't want to do that would have—that he would have done if we had provided these people with the ability to defend themselves rather than be slaughtered by the most modern equipment that the Russians have.

Mr. Clapper. Well, I don't think he will view it happily if we provide—if the United States provides lethal support. That's——

Chairman McCain. Because more Russians might be killed who are now in Crimea killing Ukrainians.

Mr. CLAPPER. That's right. And it will be harder for him to hide that fact to the home audience.

Chairman MCCAIN. What difference does it make whether he hides it? There's no hiding what he's done. Everybody knows what he's done.

Mr. CLAPPER. Well, everyone in Russia——

Chairman MCCAIN. General Breedlove has made it—laid it out very clearly.

Well, I'm not in an open dispute with you. I'd—we've got to move on. But, it is just incredible to believe that he would be, quote, ''provoked'' to further action, when he has achieved every goal that he sought along the way. And we'll see who's right about Mariupol, Director Clapper.

Mr. CLAPPER. Sir, I'm not arguing about Mariupol. The only issue there is timing. I believe they will not—they'll wait——

Chairman MCCAIN. He's got plenty of time.

Mr. CLAPPER.—they'll wait til the spring before they attack. That's——

Chairman MCCAIN. Sure.

Mr. CLAPPER. That will be a formal undertaking for the Russians and the separatists.

Chairman MCCAIN. I agree with you.

Mr. CLAPPER. It's much better defended.

Chairman MCCAIN. I totally agree with you. Why not pull back? He's not getting any increasing in sanctions, he's not getting weapons—or the Ukrainians aren't receiving defensive weapons from us. If I were him, I would do exactly that, too. He's got plenty of time.

Yesterday, the Secretary of State said, ''Our citizens, our world today, is actually—despite ISIL, despite the visible killings that you see and how horrific they are, we're actually living in a period of less daily threat to Americans and to people in the world than normally. Less deaths, less violent deaths today than through the last century.'' And yet, just today, the Director of the Federal Bureau of Investigation (FBI) and others have said that there are threats to 30 nations—excuse me—30 States in this Nation. What is your view of the threat to the United States of America, Director Clapper?

Mr. CLAPPER. Well, first, sir, I will say, as I've said every year—this'll be the fifth year that—in my 50-plus years in the intelligence business, I don't know of a time that has been more beset by challenges and crises around the world. I worry a lot about the safety and security of this country, for a lot of reasons, not the least of which, which Senator Reed alluded to, is the impacts that sequestration is having on the intelligence community. We didn't get a pass. So, the same rules that apply to, say, the Department of Defense apply to us, as well. So, the combination of the challenges that we have around the world and the declining resource base that we have to monitor them is of concern to me.

Chairman MCCAIN. So, could I just——

Mr. CLAPPER. Director Comey was referring to the fact that he now has some form of investigation—and, of course, the FBI has a tiered system for intensity of investigation—and they now have some form of investigation on homegrown violent extremists, not necessarily direct sympathizers or supporters of ISIL, but in all 50 of our States.

Chairman MCCAIN. Thank you, Director. And I could just ask, again, because you made reference to it, if we don't—if we stick to sequestration, as it is planned, it will impair our ability for you to do your job and defend this Nation. Is that a correct statement?

Mr. CLAPPER. Yes, sir. And I've said that in the past. A little harder for intelligence to make that case as concretely as, say, the Navy and how many ships it builds, or the Air Force and how many aircraft it's able to fly. In our case, the impacts—I hate to use the word, but I will—are more insidious, in that predicting when we have a lesser capability will eventuate in a failure is hard to quantify. But, just based on my best professional judgment from having served in this business for a long time, I'm very concerned about it. And if we revert to sequestration in 2016, the damage to the intelligence community will be quite profound.

Chairman MCCAIN. I thank you very much, Director.

Thank you, General.

Jack?

Senator REED. General, thank you. And, both generals, thank you.

The Chairman has covered very well some of the issues arising out of the Russian activities in Ukraine and Crimea. Is your assessment that Putin is carrying out a strategic plan, or is some of this opportunistic? He's just seizing the moment? Or it's a combination of both?

Mr. CLAPPER. I'm sorry, sir, I didn't——

Senator REED. Or is it a combination of both.

Mr. CLAPPER. Both——

Senator REED. He has a strategy——

Mr. CLAPPER.—a strategic plan and——

Senator REED.—and opportunistic——

Mr. CLAPPER. Well, yes. I think it became a strategic plan when Yanukovych upped and left very suddenly last—almost a year ago, 22nd of February. And then I think he saw an opportunity, particularly with the seizure of Crimea, which I think has always been in his craw. And, given Putin's approach and the way he looks at greater Russia and what a disaster the breakup of the Soviet Union was, and his—as I said in my statement, that his highest foreign policy objective is controlling the former Soviet space. So, I think, on the heels of the seizure of Crimea and the establishment of some sort of an arrangement in eastern Ukraine, and what I believe will be more of a softer approach, maybe not direct military action, but, as the Chairman alluded to, Transnistria and Moldova, and certainly there'll be pressure brought to bear in the Baltics, particularly where there are high levels of Russian minorities. A little different situation with the Baltics, since they are North Atlantic Treaty Organization (NATO) members, which, of course, Moldova, Ukraine, et cetera, are not.

Senator REED. We have conducted recently some very small military demonstrations in the Baltics. Company of the 173rd Airborne went in. I think just a day or two ago there was a parade of U.S. military vehicles. What's the reaction to the Russians to those?

Mr. CLAPPER. Well, they, I think, watch that. I mean, that's—it's an—it's symbolically important. There's a messaging there. And I think it is—and they're sensitive to that. They're mindful of the fact that the Baltic nations are NATO members. And I do think they distinguish that.

Senator REED. We have elaborate sanctions in place. You've indicated in your comments that they have not had, in my interpretation, an appreciable effect yet on his strategy. They might be affecting the economy, but they haven't affected his strategy.

Mr. CLAPPER. That's exactly right, Senator Reed. So far, that has not changed his approach. And, of course, what's had the greater impact, frankly, on the economy has been the——

Senator REED. Oil.

Mr. CLAPPER.—precipitous drop in oil prices.

Senator REED. Do you have any sort of indication that this is— as this situation deteriorates further, there will be an impact on his strategy?

Mr. CLAPPER. There could. And there—and, of course, what we see is, they're very sensitive to opposition, you know, demonstrations in the street. They're very, very sensitive about a color revolution occurring in Russia, itself. And, of course, that's another reason why Putin reacted to the situation in Ukraine, because he believes we instigated that as another color revolution in Ukraine right on his doorstep, and that, in turn, posed a—in his mind, an existential threat to—in Russia.

Senator REED. Just changing gears, the Iranians have a explicit presence in Iraq today, and we have forces there, too. And in the next several days or weeks, there's two possible triggering events. One would be much more aggressive action against the Assad regime in Syria or the resolution of the negotiations with the Iranians on their nuclear program. Do you have any views with respect to what might happen to—within Iraq with respect to their Iranian forces, which are now sort of not cooperating with us, but——

Mr. CLAPPER. Is your question, sir, Is there a connection between the nuclear negotiations and agreement——

Senator REED. Will there be a reaction in Iraq to either the activities that we undertake, or proceed to undertake, in Syria or the conclusion of the negotiations?

Mr. CLAPPER. I really don't think that the negotiations, one way or the other, will have much bearing on what they do in Iraq or anyplace they are trying to exert their influence, meaning Syria or now Yemen. As best we can tell, the Iranians have kind of segmented the nuclear negotiations and potential nuclear agreement from their regional aspirations.

Senator REED. Thank you, General.

Chairman MCCAIN. Senator Inhofe.

Senator INHOFE. Thank you, Mr. Chairman.

I have three questions—two short ones; the other one may require going on the record.

Director Clapper, I know what your answer is, after hearing your opening statement, but, when you said, "Looking back over my now more than half century of intelligence, I've not experienced a time when we've been beset by more crisis and threats around the globe.'' And you still stand by that. And—correct?

Mr. CLAPPER. Yes, sir. And if I'm hear next year, I'll probably say it again.

Senator INHOFE. Yeah. Well, I appreciate that. You've been straightforward and honest about these things.

General Stewart, you stated, and this—that we face a more diverse and complex problem than we have experienced in our lifetimes. Still stand by that?

General STEWART. Absolutely, Senator.

Senator INHOFE. Yes. Well, now, there's an assumption, when we're out in the public, out talking to real people and away from Washington, that we, who are on this committee, know a lot of answers that we don't know. And one of them that should be a very easy answer—and I want to get something from you guys that I can stand on—when we talk about the power, in terms of the strength and number of bodies in this—in ISIL or ISIS—in September 2014, we talked about that it's been an additional some—20,000 since this all started. I think we all agree on that. But, they said it was somewhere between 20- and 31,5- fighters that were in Iraq and Syria. Now we know, since that time, it's gone beyond that. Then, in August, they talked about from 80- to 100,000. Then, in November, one of the Kurdish leaders stated that the—ISIL's military had increased to 200,000 fighters. Can you kind of give us an idea—and, number one, why it's so difficult to do, and, number two, something that we can use and quote you two as the sources?

Mr. CLAPPER. It's—from my vantage, it's unfortunate these numbers get out. For one, we don't have what I would call Census Bureau door-to-door survey accuracy or fidelity over these numbers. They're very hard to come by. We have to derive them inferentially from a number of different sources. Ergo, even when we do come out with numbers, they're—you'll have a wide range. So, the current estimate is—that we're standing on, here, is somewhere in the range between 20- and 32,000 fighters. Now, the difficulty here is assessing who's a core fighter who does this full-time, who may be a facilitator or supporter and do it part time, and all that sort of thing.

I will say that the—this is one effect of the airstrikes, has been substantial attrition. They lost at least 3,000 fighters in Khobani. For whatever reason, they wanted to do that. And, as well, what that's driving them to—now we're seeing evidence of conscription. So, the estimate that we're going with——

Senator INHOFE. But, that's——

Mr. CLAPPER.—right now, but this is very dynamic, is 20- to 32,000.

Senator INHOFE. Yeah. We're—gosh, I—well, anyway.

It may take a while to get into this, but I am—I'm very much—I was over in the Ukraine when they had their elections. And that's when they had the elections, and it was Yatsenyuk as much as Poroshenko. They were just elated. Both of them from different political parties, but the political parties are very pro-Western, and they were rejoicing in the fact that, for the first time in 96 years, the Communists don't have one seat in Parliament. To me, I thought, when that happened, there's not going to be any problem with us going in with weapons. And obviously, the Democrats and Republicans up here agreed with that. We have language in our last defense authorization bill that we had $75 million, where we were encouraging the President to use, through the European Re-assurance Initiative, for weapons going in to be of assist to our best friend in that area.

Now, I can't figure out why we don't do it. Let me just ask the two of you. Would you recommend it?

Mr. CLAPPER. Sir, I think I have to answer two ways, here. One, institutionally, this is a policy issue. And——

Senator INHOFE. Yeah, now——

Mr. CLAPPER.—the Intelligence Community doesn't——

Senator INHOFE.—let me make sure. I'm not talking about sending troops, I'm talking about sending lethal weapons.

Mr. CLAPPER. I understand. I understand——

Senator INHOFE. All right.

Mr. CLAPPER.—what you're asking, and that's what I'm answering, I think. So, from an intelligence community perspective, that is a policy issue. We're down in the engine room, shoveling intelligence coal, and the people up on the bridge, to use a Navy metaphor, drive the ship and rearrange the deck chairs.

I have a personal view. And it is only that——

Senator INHOFE. All right.

Mr. CLAPPER.—that I would favor it. But, that's a personal perspective, and——

Senator INHOFE. That's what——

Mr. CLAPPER.—it does not——

Senator INHOFE. And I appreciate your——

Mr. CLAPPER.—represent an official company policy of the Intelligence Community.

Senator INHOFE. I appreciate that very much.

And General Stewart?

General STEWART. Sir, I'm trying to stay out of the personal——

Senator INHOFE. I know you're trying to stay out, but——

General STEWART. So——

Senator INHOFE.—it's time that we—we've got to get this done.

General STEWART.—we stand by the assessment, that lethal aid couldn't be delivered quickly enough or change the military balance of power on the ground.

Senator INHOFE. So, you're for lethal, right?

General STEWART. It would not change the military balance of power, and it couldn't get there quickly enough to make a difference, and that Russia will up that——

Senator INHOFE. As a military guy, do you buy this argument that we might be provoking negative reaction from Putin? You know, I listen to—I see what our—what the President is doing on—every once in a while. And they talk about, "Well, we don't want to make the terrorists mad at us, they might hurt us." And, you know—so, what's your opinion about this statement on provoking a negative reaction from Putin?

General STEWART. I think as important as Moscow placed on Ukraine to keep it in their near abroad, to keep it out of the EU, to keep it out of NATO, I think they will up the ante if we do any lethal aid or take any actions to bolster the Ukrainians. Whether that provokes the President or not, it's hard for me to say. The realities are, they see this as central to their foreign policy, they see it as critical that they keep Ukraine out of NATO, to keep it out of the Western sphere of influence——

Senator INHOFE. Yeah, and——

General STEWART.—and exert influence. And they'll react accordingly, I suspect.

Senator INHOFE. Thank you, General.

Chairman MCCAIN. Well, I'm sure that Hitler felt the same way, General Stewart, about the Sudetenland, about German-speaking people. I'm sure he felt exactly the same way that Vladimir Putin does. And, for you to say that we can't get lethal weapons there quickly enough, that defies logic, General. I know how we can transport weapons. We can put 'em on aircraft and fly 'em over there.

General STEWART. But, you——

Chairman MCCAIN. How do you justify a statement like that?

General STEWART. Senator, I believe the answer was, "We couldn't deliver lethal aid sufficiently—quickly enough to change the military balance of power on the ground." And I think I stand——

Chairman MCCAIN. Quickly enough? What does that mean? I—it's——

General STEWART. Russia and the separatists have significant interior lines that they can resupply a lot faster with a lot heavier weapons than we could deliver in—so, it would be a race to see who could arm. And I think, with their interior lines, they would have a significant advantage on the ground.

Chairman MCCAIN. I'm sure that the Russians had a significant advantage when they invaded Afghanistan. I'm sure that, throughout history, when we've helped people who have been invaded and oppressed, and when we haven't, what is—the consequences have been. Very disappointing, General.

Senator Shaheen.

Senator SHAHEEN. Thank you, Mr. Chairman.

And thank you both for your testimony.

I want to go back to the Middle East and to what's happening in Syria. To what extent is Assad's continued—I don't want to say "control over Syria," because I appreciate that he doesn't have control over the entire country—but, to what extent is his position there an obstacle to our fight against ISIL? And is there—what's the thinking about how to change that dynamic?

Mr. CLAPPER. Well, I—that—the last part of your question is a tough one. I—he maintains the control because of his control of the economic levers, to the extent that they have them. His focus is on the—what I would call the "Western spine," say from Aleppo to Damascus. That's where most of the population is, and the major commercial entities, to include the ports. So, he has surrounded by people who are committed to preserving that, because they benefit from it. They are the minority. The Alawites are, you know, only 10 percent. So, for them, this is an existential struggle. And, of course, the irony is that we actually are in common in—both Assad and his regime are opposed to and fighting ISIL, as we are. And so, it's a very, you know, complex array of factors there.

Senator SHAHEEN. And to what extent have—has that affected other Arab countries in the Middle East and their willingness to engage with us?

Mr. CLAPPER. Well, there's been, you know, I think, somewhat of a change. It's gradual. But, the fact that many of these countries aren't participating in the coalition that General John Allen has been organizing. I do think the brutal savagery of the ISIL, and the beheadings and then the emulation of the Jordanian pilot, have had a galvanizing effect on opinion in the Mideast region. So, I think there is more of a willingness to cooperate. There certainly is, from the standpoint of intelligence sharing and our partnering with our counterparts in that part of the world.

Senator SHAHEEN. And are you optimistic that Turkey will become more engaged than they have been?

Mr. CLAPPER. No, I'm not. I think Turkey has other priorities and other interests. They are more focused on what they consider to be the threat: the KGK, the Kurdish resistance, if you will, in Turkey. Public opinion polls show, in Turkey, they don't see ISIL as a primary threat. They're more focused internally on their economy and this sort of thing. And, of course, the consequence of that is a permissive environment, in terms of—because of their laws, and the ability of people to travel through Turkey en route to Syria. So, somewhere in the neighborhood of 60 percent of those foreign fighters find their way to Syria through Turkey.

Senator SHAHEEN. And to move to Iraq, to what extent is Iran's presence in Iraq an obstacle to Abadi's ability to make the kinds of overtures and engage the Sunnis in the way that he needs to in——

Mr. CLAPPER. Well, he—he's in a very——

Senator SHAHEEN.—order to keep the country unified?

Mr. CLAPPER.—very difficult position, having to balance these competing constituencies. And clearly the Iranians have influence. They're there. They're helping, as well, in the fight against ISIL. He's got issues with his own Shi'a power base, since they're competitors to him. There's still great reluctance to fully include the Sunnis, which must happen. There are two laws in their Council of Representatives that are extremely important to Sunnis: de-Ba'athification and——

Senator SHAHEEN. Right.

Mr. CLAPPER.—anti-terrorism laws. So, he's in a very, very difficult position.

Senator SHAHEEN. What I'm trying to ask you to respond to, and I haven't been as articulate as I should, I guess, is, To what extent does—is Iran weighing their efforts to under—to take on ISIL versus the Sunni's role in Iraq? I mean, are they balancing that? Are they just——

Mr. CLAPPER. Well, the fundamental interest of the Iranians, of course, is to preserve a Shi'a or Shi'a-friendly government in Baghdad. So, that is kind of their underlying policy objective. And, of course, ISIL poses a threat to the Iranians, as well. And so, they have an interest there in sustaining their aggressive combat, if you will, and assistance in opposing ISIL.

Senator SHAHEEN. My time is up. Thank you both.

Chairman MCCAIN. Senator Ernst.

Senator ERNST. Thank you, Mr. Chairman.

Thank you, gentlemen, for appearing before us today. I do appreciate your service.

I'd like to go into the discussion with Iran a little bit more. Their Iranian military is arguably one of the most deployed forces in the Middle East from—in probably more than a generation. But, they have been into areas, such as Syria, Iraq, Lebanon, Bahrain, Yemen. So, Iran is effectively reinforcing and increasing its sphere of influence in the region. And it is also defending its allies in ways which afford Iran the ability to decisively engage its adversaries and immediately alter any battlefield momentum. So, we have seen a progression of expert witnesses in front of this very panel, and many of my colleagues and these witnesses have stated that they do believe the President is failing in this area of setting a national strategy. And his failure to construct a comprehensive strategy against Iran has led to Iran's expanded influence in the Middle East.

So, I would like to hear your assessment, Director Clapper, on, of course, the tools that Iran has in its pocket, and whether we are effectively engaging Iran, what we need to do to gain a national security strategy. I'd like to see all the pieces put together, please.

Mr. CLAPPER. Well, I can—Senator, I can comment on the intelligence aspects of this. national security strategy, again, is not my compartment.

But, the way that Iran is exerting its influence, I think, most prominently in the region is through the—their organization called the Iranian Republican Guard Corps, Quds Force, which is a combination of intelligence and special ops, has extensive commercial enterprise businesses, and this sort of thing. And so, they use that as their instrumentality, as they are now in Iraq, for extending their influence, as one of their proxies. And, of course, another one of their proxies is the Hezbollah, which they have had a long client-subordinate relationship with. And so, they use those as sort of the physical manifestation of their spreading their influence in the region. And, certainly from an intelligence perspective, we—you know, we try hard to keep tabs on those entities as we can from intelligence.

Senator ERNST. And is there a way, Director, that we can more effectively engage our neighbors in the Middle East to push back on Iran's influence?

Mr. CLAPPER. Well, we—from an intelligence perspective, which is all I can speak to, we do engage with our intelligence counterparts in all of these countries, those who are willing to engage with us, particularly the Sunni countries, who also—who do harbor great reservations about Iranians—Iranian objectives.

Senator ERNST. Thank you very much.

I'll yield back my time.

Chairman MCCAIN. Senator Donnelly.

Senator DONNELLY. Thank you, Mr. Chairman.

And thank you both for being here.

In regards to Iraq, what do you think are the biggest challenges that the Iraqi forces face right now in pushing ISIS back from Mosul and Tikrit?

Mr. CLAPPER. Well, a first thing, I think—and General Stewart can speak to this as well, since he's——

Senator DONNELLY. Right.

Mr. CLAPPER.—served there—but, obviously, the Iraqi Security Forces, particularly the army, need to reconstitute, after the precipitate losses in northern Iraq last June, where about four-and-a-half divisions or so of Iraqi forces just kind of melted away. So, that is—first order of business, I think, is to reconstitute them, which includes training and, hopefully, instantiation of a will to fight. They have challenges, clearly, with command and control, with leadership, with logistics. So, they've got a whole range of issues there that need to be attended to before they'd be in a position to, certainly unilaterally, retake a—you know, a place like——

Senator DONNELLY. General, how long do you think that'll take, to try to get them back up to speed?

General STEWART. So, if I could put it in context, last fall they had about 185,000 in the Iraqi Security Force, about three divisions—the 6th, the 9th, and the 7th Division. All three of those divisions are engaged today, so they're not getting that continuous training. They're engaged in operations. They're building three additional divisions. Those three divisions, you're talking about building from the ground up. So, to build from the ground up individual soldiers——

Senator DONNELLY. When are they ready?

General STEWART. We're talking probably 6 to 9 months, at a best estimate.

Senator DONNELLY. Director Clapper, here at home, when I look at what's going on with ISIS and see the threats that occur here, and the threat levels that we had last year—if you had to put it in perspective—this time last year, this time now—and it's an inexact art, percentagewise—significantly increased threats now than we were having last year at this same time, about the same?

Mr. CLAPPER. It's probably about the same, sir.

Senator DONNELLY. Okay. And in regards to ISIS—so, our push is to get 'em out of Iraq, then to remove them from Syria—when we get to that point where ISIS is gone, does that threat level come down, here at home?

Mr. CLAPPER. It would—I—yeah, absolutely it would, I think, but—at least that would reduce the threat some. But, again, as—if the caliphate is extended to other locations, which is what ISIL is trying to do—Libya, Egypt, et cetera—then we'll have that to contend with. So, yes, there would be some reduction of threat because—if ISIL were defeated in both Iraq and Syria, at least you are—have done away with a substantial safe haven, which would serve to reduce the threat some.

Senator DONNELLY. When you look over to Libya, is that the next place, or one of the key places, they look now as, ''Here's open space that's failed. Here's a place where we can try to grow''?

Mr. CLAPPER. It is probably the most troublesome, from that standpoint, just because of the conditions in Libya—you know, two competing governments fighting with each other. There are, in addition to ISIL, probably six or eight other terrorist groups that have gathered in Libya. So, it's a magnet because of—essentially, it's ungoverned.

Senator DONNELLY. And when you look at a place that's ungoverned, you know, not too far from the Mediterranean, right there, what do you see—like you said, you don't set all the strategy; you review all the intelligence—but, what do you see as the best steps we can take in that region right now—and, General Stewart, you, too—in Libya, to try to change the course of what's going on?

Mr. CLAPPER. Well, from an intelligence perspective we, I think, clearly need to step up our game from an ISR perspective, where we can operate. I think there's a lot of merit to partnering with the French, who have sort of staked out their claim in the Sahel region of North Africa. So, we have worked with the French, particularly from an intelligence perspective, to share with them. They have history and heritage there, access, and have committed to deploying troops in that area—boots on the ground, which we can supplement. So, those are things, from an intelligence perspective, that we—so, as we get a better handle on just what is going on in that part of the world.

Senator DONNELLY. And I see my time is up, but I just want to ask one very quick question that you can just——

How are we doing on cooperation, interagency, here at home? Better than ever before?

Mr. CLAPPER. Well, that's, frankly, the reason my job was created, after September 11, is—promote integration here in this country. I'd like to think it's better. I was around for a long time before September 11, so I—it is better, but it's—there was always improvement. We're not as mature in the—on the domestic side, in coordinating with State, local, tribal, et cetera, but I think we've made a lot of progress there, and we'll continue. And it's something I push very hard.

Senator DONNELLY. Thank you, Mr. Chairman.

Chairman MCCAIN. Senator Fischer.

Senator FISCHER. Thank you, Mr. Chairman.

Director Clapper, what do you assess is Assad's likely response to the introduction of our United States-trained Syrians to move in against ISIL in Syria? And do you assess that Assad will attack them?

Mr. CLAPPER. Well, if the—as long as Assad is—believes somehow that this—once it gets up sufficient center of mass, you know, enough force—as long as he felt as though this were something to be used only against ISIL, he'd probably be okay with it. But, I think he'd have a hard time determining whether it's a threat to ISIL or a threat to him. So, I could see a circumstance where, depending on what information he's getting—and we wonder about that sometimes—that he could easily consider that force as a threat to him.

Senator FISCHER. Do you believe that you're receiving good intelligence from that—from Syria, from that area, in regards to this?

Mr. CLAPPER. No, we have a lot of gaps for—intelligence gaps in Syria, principally because we're not there. So, no, I'm not satisfied with that. We're working at it, obviously, to come up with more intelligence from Syria. But, that's a tough problem for us.

Senator FISCHER. Have you received any intelligence that would, I guess, give you comfort, in that the moderates that would be trained by us would, in fact, be fighting ISIL and not Assad?

Mr. CLAPPER. I think a more fulsome response to that would be best in a classified environment. But, I guess the short answer would be yes.

Senator FISCHER. Okay. And how do you—how would you assess Russia and Iran will be looking at these trained forces?

Mr. CLAPPER. Well, probably wouldn't like it. I think, at this point, you know, Russia looks at Syria as a client, as an ally, some-one that they provide support to. So, again, it would be almost the same perception problem with the Russians as it would be with Assad. If—they could probably rationalize, if it's focused on ISIL, but if it be—it's perceived as a threat to the regime, then I think that they would react negatively to it.

Senator FISCHER. And if they would perceive it as a threat, what type of force would they employ, then? You said they'd react nega-tively.

Mr. CLAPPER. The Russians?

Senator FISCHER. Yes.

Mr. CLAPPER. I'd—well, I—this is really speculative, hypo-thetical. I don't think they would necessarily deploy combat forces to Syria. They would probably step up military equipment support, which they've been doing, intelligence support, if, in fact, they, too, perceive that what we were doing was a direct threat to Assad.

Senator FISCHER. Okay. And if I could shift gears, here, I'd like to ask you something about cybersecurity. As you know, the Senate is looking at a bill to authorize greater information sharing. There are some concerns out there about the entities that the—that we might be sharing that information with. I'd like to ask you, How do we balance that? How do we balance the risks between really valuable information sharing and the need not to provide informa-tion either to private individuals, hackers that are out there, or to a foreign government that may be able to pick up information that we give our colleagues, in trying to work with this, that they could then, in turn, use against us?

Mr. CLAPPER. Well, that's exactly the issue. In fact, that's a gen-eral dilemma that we have across the board, whether it's cyber or any other dimension. You know, the—sharing versus security. And that's the same issue here. There is no silver-bullet answer here.

I do think there, though, needs to be some form of legislation that would protect, from a liability standpoint, commercial concerns so that they would more freely—they'd be in a position to share with the government. This is not something government can do all by itself. There has to be—given the pervasiveness of cyber in our society, we must have the partnering of the civilian sector, which means promoting sharing, both ways.

But, you're right, there's always this concern, there's always a tradeoff between security and sharing.

Senator FISCHER. Thank you, sir.

Chairman MCCAIN. Senator King.

Senator KING. Thank you, Mr. Chairman.

To follow up on that, I believe that it's critically important that we move legislation that provides for that sharing so that we have more vigorous defense. And, indeed, the Intelligence Committee reported out a bill last summer. I understand that that bill has been somewhat renegotiated, reworked, and it will be moving forward reasonably soon. I hope that that's one of the Congress's highest priorities. I don't know how many warnings we have to have.

Turning to ISIS, what are the chances that it will wear out its welcome within the areas where it is now trying to govern, because of the weight of its brutal and harsh ideology? And I guess the followup question is, Do we have any intelligence about what's going on inside Mosul, inside Raqqa, in terms of the citizens and how they feel about the—this new regime?

Mr. CLAPPER. Senator King, to answer the question, I think that is a very important point, and we are seeing anecdotal evidence of resentment, and even resistance, in those areas that are controlled by ISIL, because of their brutal approach to enforcing Sharia.

I think the challenge—and we're already seeing indications of this—that ISIL has—as I mentioned in my oral statement, assuming some of the accouterments are some of the characteristics of a nation-state, and now they've having challenges with governance— they do not have enough financial wherewithal to provide the services—municipal services that are required to run a city of a million people. So, we're——

Senator KING. You mean they're running——

Mr. CLAPPER.—electricity——

Senator KING. You mean they're running a deficit? Maybe we could ship them the sequester in a sealed railroad car. [Laughter.]

Mr. CLAPPER. That'd be good.

We're seeing signs of electrical—electricity outages, shortages of food and commodities. The airstrikes against their—the refining capability has forced them to go to a lot of individual mom-and-pop refining stills. So, they're going to have trouble generating the revenue that would be needed to actually run the areas they have captured. And that—and we're seeing anecdotal evidence of the strains and the stresses that's putting particularly on the city of Mosul and its citizens.

Senator KING. Does that suggest that perhaps a containment strategy instead of a reinvasion strategy—General Stewart, you've testified recently about the proportion of troops it takes to root somebody out of an urban setting. Could you articulate that for us?

General STEWART. If I recall, we talked about the ratio of offensive forces to——

Senator KING. Correct.

General STEWART.—take a urban environment, something in an order of 10 to 1, offense versus a defense. That requires a very skilled, determined force to take that kind of action.

There is something to be said about ISIL wearing out its welcome. It's precisely what turned al Qaeda in Iraq before—the brutality, the inability to govern—that convinced the tribes that there may be a better option.

Senator KING. And ISIS is much more brutal than—and difficult than al-Qaeda, as I understand.

General STEWART. The question is, Where is the tipping point? And it's very hard to determine where that tipping point where, where the Sunnis in Anbar will go, "This is enough. There's a different option, and we ought to counter ISIS.'' So, I think there will be a tipping point at some point. We just don't know where that will be.

Senator KING. But, a—as you just testified, a 10-to-1 ratio of offense to defense going into a city like Mosul means you're going to have a large, well-trained force. And it's just a question of whether that's going to be necessary, rather than let it fall of its own weight. And I guess that's a question of timing.

General STEWART. It's a question of timing, yes, sir.

Senator KING. Quick question on cyber. It concerns me that all of our discussions about cyber are essentially defensive. We're talking about legislation to share information, we're talking about greater rebutting of these kinds of intrusions. Should we think, Mr. Director, about developing an offensive capability to provide a deterrent? It concerns me that now a—particularly a state actor can act essentially without fear of consequences. Whereas, the theory of deterrence in our nuclear field stood the test of time for 75 years. Should we think about a deterrent capacity so that people know that if they attack us in any kind of critical way, they're going to suffer in return?

Mr. CLAPPER. Yes, we—I agree with you, Senator King. We—and we do—you know, we do have offensive capabilities that I can't go into here. I think the issue, though, is, What is the policy? What is it that would achieve cyber deterrence? And that is an issue that, at the policy level, we're still, frankly, wrestling with.

Senator KING. But, it is one that—I'm delighted to hear that it is being wrestled with, and I think I heard you say that this is something that we need to consider. And, of course, to go back to Dr. Strangelove, if you have a deterrent and don't tell people about it, it's not a deterrent.

Mr. CLAPPER. Well, that's true.

Senator KING. Thank you.

Thank you, Mr. Chairman.

Chairman MCCAIN. Senator Ayotte.

Senator AYOTTE. I want to thank the Chairman, thank both of you for what you do to protect the country.

And I wanted to ask about Iran. And I know that in, your written testimony, you have said—and you previously testified, Director Clapper, before this committee, that Iran was on track, by this year, in terms of its ICBM program. So, since the negotiations have been ongoing on the nuclear program, has Iran continued to develop its ICBM program? And can you tell me what the status and the goal of that program would be from Iran?

Mr. CLAPPER. The Iranians have continued on their space launch vehicle program, and recently put into orbit a satellite. And obviously, that—any work they do on missile—missiles could conceivably go towards work on an intercontinental ballistic missile. And it's going to be hard to determine whether a given missile is launched for the purposes of a space launch vehicle, a satellite they want to put into space. Because if they do that, they also acquire proficiency, expertise, and experience in what could be a—an ICBM. And so, it's a hard question to answer, because it has a lot to do with intent. But, there's no question they have the technical competence.

Senator AYOTTE. Do you think they have good intent, in terms of what they're doing with their missile program?

Mr. CLAPPER. Well, it's—no. I mean, I think the huge medium-range ballistic missile force they have today that's operational is—you know, I think poses a threat to the region now. So——

Senator AYOTTE. And if they——

Mr. CLAPPER.—no, it's not.

Senator AYOTTE. And if they were to get ICBM capability, that obviously poses a threat, in terms of our country, and the East Coast in particular.

Mr. CLAPPER. Well, it could. I mean, it, again, depends on what they actually do. If they actually are able to—you know, it's theoretically possible they could attempt to launch one this year. So, this is something we just have to watch. But, again, the challenge for us is going to be, you know, determining just what their intent is.

Senator AYOTTE. Could you help me understand also, as we think about Iran's activities, what types of other activities they're engaging in to establish regional hegemony?

Mr. CLAPPER. Well, they are certainly trying to, where they can, reach out diplomatically. The organization that we watch a lot is the IRGC Quds Force that I mentioned previously, their intelligence activities throughout the region. But, they will look to establish their influence by whatever mechanism they can.

Senator AYOTTE. So, as I understand it, obviously they continue to support Assad, they have continued to support groups in the region, including Hezbollah. What other activities—are they still—would you still characterize them as one of the largest state sponsors of terrorism in the world?

Mr. CLAPPER. They are still classified that way, yes.

Senator AYOTTE. Thank you.

I would like to follow up on an issue that is hitting us at home, but I think has international implications, and that is of the international drug trafficking that's occurring. And, in particular, my home State of New Hampshire, we've had a devastating number of people who are dying from heroin overdoses. And so, I would certainly like to hear your opinion, General Stewart, about what is happening, in terms of drug trafficking—in particular, heroin—and how is—are the networks that are being used for drug trafficking, are they also being used to fuel terrorism?

So, General Stewart, if you could share that with me. And I'd be curious, Does Southern Command and Northern Command—what do they need, in terms of fighting heroin and also the drug trafficking that can be used to fuel terrorism, as well?

General STEWART. I'll have to look at the numbers again, but I don't think drug trafficking is on the increase from our—through our southern borders. I think Pakistan and Afghanistan heroin production continues about at the norm that we've seen over the last several years. We've seen no indications that the drug trafficking routes are being used for terrorist activities or hostile actions. And I spoke recently to the folks down in Southern Command, and I don't recall any request for additional capability to help them with the problem in the south.

Mr. CLAPPER. If I can add, Senator.

Senator AYOTTE. Yes.

Mr. CLAPPER. I well recall, I think it was last year, when General Kelly, Commander of SOUTHCOM, testified with then-General Jacoby, who was the NORTHCOM Commander—they testified together. And one of the challenges with drug trafficking is not so much a lack of intelligence—we have a lot of intelligence on it—is the lack of resource, particularly in the case of the ability to interdict, by the Coast Guard and others. And that, since General Kelly's testimony, has been—is being addressed. I've spoken—discussed that with the Commandant of the Coast Guard, and we are putting more of his capability, deploying more ships and planes, in the southern hemisphere.

But, I think I would take, you know, a little mild disagreement, here, with Vince, that I think this is a—it is a problem, the—throughout this region, not only across the border, but through Puerto Rico is another vulnerability we have. And so—and we have pretty good intelligence on this.

I think the challenge has been—and again, sequestration has had impacts—is on the ability to react and interdict.

Senator AYOTTE. I thank both of you. And I also noticed that, in your testimony, Director Clapper, you noted the incredible surge of heroin-related deaths since 2007. So, thank you. It's a horrible problem.

Senator Reed [presiding]: Senator Kaine.

Senator KAINE. Thank you, Mr. Chairman.

And thank you both for your testimony, both earlier in the week and today. Mindful that this is a—not a classified hearing, a few questions.

My perception of the level of American and allied intelligence about the extent of the Iranian nuclear program is that, before November 2013 and the beginning of the Joint Plan of Action (JPOA), the level of intelligence was good. Certainly there were gaps and challenges, but at least, if I go by public reports, the level of intelligence at—that all have, together, enabled some actions that have slowed the Iranian program.

One of the reasons I supported the JPOA is my assumption that our intel sources haven't gone away, but the inspections that were allowed—required under the JPOA, together with existing intel sources, would even give us a better level of intel, which would (a) help us determine if we needed, God forbid, to take military action to stop the program, and (b) enable us to better target any military action if, God forbid, we should need to take it. Am I looking at this the right way?

Mr. CLAPPER. Yes, sir, I think you are. I will tell you that the, you know, huge—that the important aspect of any sort of agreement we might reach with the Iranians would be a very invasive and thorough surveillance and inspection capability on the part of International Atomic Energy Agency (IAEA). I think that would be requisite to any kind of an agreement.

I—you know, we have, I think, a reasonably capable intelligence capability, but I wouldn't want to rely on it, only, for verification that, in fact, the terms of the agreement were being lived up to.

Senator KAINE. And, Director Clapper, I agree with the last point you made, is—I would look at any final deal, if one is reached, in analyzing its content and determining whether I support it or not. The degree of inspections, to me, is the key factor, because that, combined with existing intel, is our guarantee of an ability to (a) know if there's going to be a problem, and (b) take appropriate action—target an appropriate action to eliminate the problem.

You indicated, Director Clapper, in earlier testimony, that your intel suggests that Iran is looking at the nuclear negotiation as sort of separate from this whole question of Iranian bellicosity and adventurism in the region, that these are sort of separate items. My sense is, there is at least one connection between the two. And this also bears on my analysis of any deal, if reached. And that is this. Any deal, if reached, would involve sanctions relief—i.e., dollars to Iran. And they use dollars to carry out adventurism. I think—you know, just from what I've heard, some of the sanctions relief already may have enabled them to invest more heavily in running Syria as a puppet state or invest more heavily in the Quds Force or other agents that are destabilizing governments outside of their own borders. And so, to at least that extent, as we look at any deal, if there is such a deal, there could be a connection between a deal and Iranian bellicosity outside their borders.

Mr. CLAPPER. Perhaps, sir. And, in a classified environment, I can go into this a little bit more. But, the sanctions have had impacts on—financial impacts on the Iranians, and it—that, in turn, has impacted funding for the military and for even the Quds Force. So, I——

Senator KAINE. Yeah.

Mr. CLAPPER.—perhaps best left to a classified environment for——

Senator KAINE. Thank you.

Mr. CLAPPER.—more details.

Senator KAINE. We have had two meetings of the Senate Foreign Relations Committee, in the last 3 weeks, where we've heard from leaders from the region who are engaged in the fight against ISIL. King Abdullah was with us about 3 weeks ago, and he told us, in a coffee at the Foreign Relations Committee, that American ground troops as part of this battle of ISIL would not be a good idea, in his view. Yesterday, we had a coffee with the Emir of Qatar, Sheikh Tamim, who also said American ground troops is a bad idea because it would convert the perception of the battle against ISIL to the United States or west against ISIL rather than, ''We are engaging in a battle to clean up our own regional extremists. And we want the—we want America's help on that.'' But, they both offered us advice that American ground troops would be problematic, because it would enable, from a propaganda standpoint, this being positioned as American or Western occupation, and that America is the point of the sphere—the spear against that terrorist threat. I'd just report that to you, and I would be curious to either of your's—your reactions to those comments from trusted allies.

Mr. CLAPPER. Well, the—I have had similar discussions with the King, and he is a staunch proponent, an articulate one, for, you know, ''the people in the region have to take this on and have to lead,'' and that, you know, the United States—anytime we show up someplace, then, you know, we're a—we're, by definition, occupiers. He—you know, he recognizes, as do many others, that, at some point, there will be a need for boots on the ground, but hopefully others, not the United States, because that engenders its own challenges and issues.

Senator KAINE. Thank you.

Thank you, Mr. Chairman.

Senator REED. Senator Sessions.

Senator SESSIONS. Thank you, Senator Reed.

And just to follow up on Senator Kaine's comment, I think we need to reestablish where we are, or confirm where we are, not—Director Clapper, is it still our policy that no options are off the table and that Iran should not have a nuclear weapon?

Mr. CLAPPER. That's my understanding, yes, sir.

Senator SESSIONS. That's your understanding. Do you have any doubt about it?

Mr. CLAPPER. I take what the administration said for its word, that all options are not—no options are off the table.

Senator SESSIONS. Well, I think that's true. We had a very important hearing yesterday on nuclear forces and strategic forces. And one of the things I came away with was greater concerns than I had before about the proliferation impacts, the instability in the region that could occur from a nuclear-armed Iran. And I just think that we've got to be careful about that. And I do remember that the CIA reported, in, what, early 2000s, that Iran wasn't intent on building a nuclear weapon. That was wrong, was it not?

Mr. CLAPPER. Well, up until 2003, they were. Right now, they—and, of course, the—we believe the Supreme Leader would be the ultimate decisionmaker, here. And, as far as we know, he's not made a decision to go for a nuclear weapon. I do think that they certainly want to preserve options across the capabilities it would take to field one, but right now they don't have one, and have not made that decision.

Senator SESSIONS. Well, we've been——

Mr. CLAPPER. But, I agree with you, it would be very—it would be very profound and very destabilizing if they were to achieve a nuclear weapon.

Senator SESSIONS. Is—I mean, it really makes us face some really tough choices. Our—I don't—but, I don't think there's any doubt they were—they would never—they never relinquished the intention to build a weapon. The CIA report was in error. And they are closer today. And every month that goes by, it seems they get closer.

General Stewart, I had the honor to be briefed by you in 2006 or 2007 in the al-Anbar region in Iraq. And you gave us a remarkable briefing about how you had—the marines had worked with the tribal leaders, and they began The Awakening that allowed them to remove al-Qaeda from that region after great, great commitment by the marines and other forces.

This is what I would like to see. I am not for any major, massive American troop leadership in Iraq, but I do think—and I want you to give us your best judgment—but isn't it true that even a few embedded forces with the Iraqis with the ability to communicate to aircraft and bringing in smart bombs and to assist them, that that does encourage them, and that the Iranian forces fight better under those circumstances than if they don't have the confidence that a—even a small American presence with them brings?

General STEWART. Senator, let me answer the question this way. Senator Kaine raised a great point of what we've heard. The best propaganda victory that we could give ISIL is to make this a fight between the West and Islam—and ISIL. But, being able to provide ISR, precision fires, some command and control will certainly help those forces—Iraqi forces—to be much more effective on the ground than left to their own devices.

Senator SESSIONS. And—all right, I agree with that. But, I'm just asking you, from your experience with them, isn't it true that there is more confidence, even if there are just one or two Special Forces there with them—not out in the—leading the fight—

General STEWART. Right.

Senator SESSIONS.—but with the forces that are advancing?

General STEWART. There is a great sense of comfort when U.S. forces are with our partners to provide precision, to provide command and control, to help bolster leadership. There is some advantage, yes, sir.

Senator SESSIONS. With regard to the momentum that we have there, aren't there—I mean, we have a large Iraqi army. And——

Is my time up? My time's up, Mr. Chairman. Thank you. Maybe we'll——

Chairman MCCAIN [presiding]. If you want to finish your question——

Senator SESSIONS. How—are they—can't some of those divisions, some of those units, be utilized now to blunt the momentum that they have—that ISIS has achieved, and maybe take the bloom off their rose and give some confidence again, in the Iraqi forces, that they can retake the territory, and the sooner is better than later?

General STEWART. Yes, Senator. In fact, they have blunted the ISIL advance. And, best as we can guess, ISIL has lost territory over the last couple of months. So, it's not just the Iraqi Security Forces. You have the Kurdish forces that are involved. And they are making a difference. I wouldn't categorize the difference as significant, but they are, in fact, causing ISIL to lose territory at this point.

Senator SESSIONS. We've been training them for a decade. Not as if they need another—I don't know. I'm—a little odd that we need another 6 to 9 months of training, when I thought we were training the Iraqi armies for nearly a decade.

General STEWART. When we talk about the 6 to 9 months additional training, it is to deal with an urban fight, which is very, very different, very complex, requires a great deal of skill, a great deal of precision to be successful.

Senator SESSIONS. Thank you, General, in your leadership and your commitment to fight this——

Chairman MCCAIN. Also has to do with the collapse of the Iraqi army.

Senator Manchin.

Senator MANCHIN. Thank you, Mr. Chairman.

And thanks, both of you, again for being here. And just a couple of questions I have.

Following up on the Iran nuclear capabilities that they may have, since we know that they haven't dismantled—they might have downgraded some of their enriched uranium—are we just prolonging the inevitable? I mean, they're going to be able to get up to enrichment and to armament speed pretty quickly, if they desired, unless there's an absolute dismantlement of their——

Mr. CLAPPER. Well——

Senator MANCHIN.—capabilities. Director Clapper?

Mr. CLAPPER.—that's obviously the concern, and that's why the importance of intrusive and comprehensive surveillance and inspection is so critical, to make sure they don't, particularly, enrich to highly enriched uranium.

Senator MANCHIN. But, we're not doing away with any of their centrifuges. They're not downgrading some of the things that they can, or taking away their capabilities. I don't think our agreement's——

Mr. CLAPPER. Well, that's——

Senator MANCHIN.—going to achieve that.

Mr. CLAPPER.—that's to be determined. That's a—you know, the—and I don't want to talk too much about this——

Senator MANCHIN. Sure.

Mr. CLAPPER.—because of the delicate state of play with the negotiations, themselves. But, that's all in play as part of the negotiations.

Senator MANCHIN. Well, I have a concern.

If I could switch gears over to China and—basically, our partners in Asia-Pacific area, especially Taiwan. They're growing uneasy about China's access area denial strategy which seeks to limit American power in that region. Can you please update us on China's effort to deny American access to the Asia-Pacific region, sir?

Mr. CLAPPER. Well, the Chinese—and I can't go into a great deal of detail here, but the Chinese are embarked on extremely impressive military modernization program across the board. And their modernization program is deliberately designed to counteract or thwart what they feel are our strengths; meaning carrier aviation, our bases, C4ISR, and our abilities in space. And they are doing specific things in each one of those realms to deny us, first, potentially, surveillance, command and control, as well as what they view is our primary weapons—our primary strengths. I can certainly go into—in more detail if you're—if you'd like, in a classified setting.

Senator MANCHIN. Okay. I'm just—I guess you're not able to speak about their developing capabilities within the last 10 years or what they're accelerating. I'm understanding they're accelerating very fastly. You said they're impressive.

Mr. CLAPPER. They are. And they also are getting more and more into the realm of indigenously designing and producing things, rather than relying on others, notably the Russians.

Senator MANCHIN. Okay. Let me see, I had one more here for you.

We talked about, I think, in a closed setting—you might be able to talk about it in generality here—as far as ISIS, their ability, as far as financial ability, to attract the dollars they do, be able to operate the way they can. And are we having any success in shutting down that money flow?

Mr. CLAPPER. Well, they—again, I'll have to speak in generalities, here—they acquired a lot of funding initially, some of which was derived from overrunning Iraqi banks.

Senator MANCHIN. Sure.

Mr. CLAPPER. That's going to dry up. And, of course, the air-strikes against the oil has made that—forced them to go to sort of mom-and-pop stills. And, as a consequence of the brutality, the donations that they've received are tapering off. So, I think, again, this says something about an attrition——

Senator MANCHIN. I——

Mr. CLAPPER.—approach which I think, over time—and the other thing, of course, that's draining resources is the demands that they have for governance, particularly in large——

Senator MANCHIN. Yeah.

Mr. CLAPPER.—cities like Mosul.

Senator MANCHIN. Just a—just very quickly. But, the rapid rise, as far as in their—when we first heard about ISIS, it was 3-, 5,000, then it just seemed to leapfrog to 10-, 15-, 20-, and 30-. Were they paying their soldiers, or attracting because of better pay than—

Mr. CLAPPER. The reason they——

Senator MANCHIN.—al Qaeda and Taliban?

Mr. CLAPPER. The reason they—there was sort of mushrooming growth there, and the initial phases when they did their attacks in northern Iraq——

Senator MANCHIN. Sure.

Mr. CLAPPER.—was because the—this is largely a Sunni region. They were very receptive, frankly, to joining up with ISIL, which I think many viewed as a better protector of themselves and their communities and their families than were the Iraqi Government. So, that's what occasioned the joining up.

Senator MANCHIN. Do you have any——

Mr. CLAPPER. Now, we're—we're now seeing anecdotal evidence of their having—and paid, you know, money——

Senator MANCHIN. Were they paying better than——

Mr. CLAPPER. They are——

Senator MANCHIN.—everybody else?

Mr. CLAPPER.—also having to reduce the amount of money they're paying some of their fighters.

Senator MANCHIN. So, that should reduce—that could reduce some of their strength, right? If they don't pay them as well as somebody else?

Mr. CLAPPER. That and the—and what we're also seeing—again, anecdotal evidence of—they've been driven to conscription. In other worse, forcing people to join the ranks to——

Senator MANCHIN. Gotcha.

Mr. CLAPPER.—sustain their fighter force, particularly as they've taken some pretty heavy losses—notably, in Khobani.

Senator MANCHIN. Thank you, Mr. Chair.

Chairman MCCAIN. Senator Sullivan.

Senator SULLIVAN. Thank you, gentlemen, for your wonderful service to our country.

General Stewart, you may have noticed the Chairman has a particularly soft spot in his heart for marines. He's probably treated you in that regard. So——

General STEWART. I'm pretty delighted about that, too, Senator.

Senator SULLIVAN. Yeah. Well, I'll make sure he keeps treating you with kid gloves, I'm sure.

I want to thank you gentlemen for what you're doing, because I think that your service, particularly providing real, accurate threat assessments to not only the Congress, but to the American people, the administration, is absolutely, fundamentally critical if we're going to get a hold of these—many of the challenges that we face right now as a country. And you probably noticed that this committee has had several hearings over the last several weeks about these assessments with some luminaries, Democrat, Republican, former Secretaries of State, former four-star generals, about what they see as some of the challenges and strategies that we need. I think there was consensus that we're living in a very challenging environment. Henry Kissinger mentioned it was one of the most challenging that he's ever seen in his career, which says a lot.

What I want to touch on a little bit is what I see as a rather disturbing disconnect between some of the testimony that comes from gentlemen like yourself from this whole series of hearings that we had and the disconnect between that and senior administration officials. Let me give you a few examples.

The President, himself, in the State of the Union, talked about the crisis of 9/11 and everything has passed. Went through a whole list of things that made it sound like we're living in a very benign world environment.

The Secretary of State yesterday talked about, ''actually living in a period of less daily threats to American and people in the world normally.'' That was his quote.

The recent National Security Strategy document from the White House lists, I believe, climate change if—as one of the top, if not the top, national security threat, relative to, say, Iran gaining nuclear weapons, or ISIS.

Do you agree with these assessments from the senior leadership of the administration, that we're living in a less daily threatening—that Iran gaining nuclear weapons is less of a threat than climate change? I really need—I think it's critical that we level with the American people what exactly are the threats that we face as a country right now. And I don't think we're getting it from the administration.

Mr. CLAPPER. Well, I think our function, in the intelligence community, is to portray, as accurately as we can, what we see as the threats. We probably always occupy the half of the glass that's empty, and policymakers, and oftentimes military commanders, will occupy the half of the glass that's full. Probably the real truth is at the water line.

I think our instinct, frankly, is to perhaps—I've been criticized for this—worst-case the situation. Having been on the receiving end of virtually every post-event critique investigating intelligence failures since September 11, I think we are much more conservative and much more cautious than others might be about the nature of the world out there. But, I think we have a certain institutional responsibility, which we try to discharge. If others don't see it that way or others don't agree, that's certainly their prerogative.

Senator SULLIVAN. So, do you agree with those assessments that——

Mr. CLAPPER. I'm not in the mode of—we don't do policy, and I'm not critiquing those who do make it.

Senator SULLIVAN. Okay. I don't think that's policy that they've been putting out. I think it's—they're giving threat assessments to the American people that are inaccurate. But, let me——

Mr. CLAPPER. Well, climate change——

Senator SULLIVAN. I'll move on——

Mr. CLAPPER. I mean, climate change, for example, I think will have—does have national security implications. It—if you watch what's going on in the Arctic now, and the impacts on climate change, in terms of water availability and this sort of thing, does have national security implications. I probably wouldn't rank it up there as problem or threat number one, but it is a serious concern.

Senator SULLIVAN. Let me just ask General Stewart. The—you know, the—Senator Manchin was talking about the increasing recruitment of ISIL. What role do you see that they are perceived as continuing to win, as continuing to be victorious, as continuing to be kind of a team that's gaining ground, not being defeated? I think—in your experience, I'm sure that if a recruit thinks he's going to go join a team and get killed, he probably is not going to be interested in joining that team, but if they seem to be perceived as kind of gaining ground—North Africa now, Syria, Iraq—do you think that that helps in their recruitment efforts?

General STEWART. A very capable propaganda media operation that emphasizes their success and their victories, however small, and that is a basis for attracting those who would move to that ideology. So, their success on the battlefield, or perceived success, or the way they're presented, certainly helps them in gaining recruits for the fight.

Senator SULLIVAN. Thank you.

Thank you, Mr. Chairman.

Chairman MCCAIN. Senator Gillibrand.

Senator GILLIBRAND. Thank you, Mr. Chairman.

Thank you both for being here today.

The execution of Coptic Christians in Libya by terrorists affiliated with ISIL raises a question about ISIL's ability to coordinate with other groups. What's your assessment of the links between ISIL in Syria and Iraq and the groups that have acted in its name outside of those two countries?

Mr. CLAPPER. If you're referring to ISIL's other chapters or provinces, so-called, if that's what you—if that's what you're referring to?

Senator GILLIBRAND. Yes.

Mr. CLAPPER. And what's the connection there?

Senator GILLIBRAND. So, what's your assessment of their ability to coordinate, to communicate, to engage in terrorist acts outside of Syria and Iraq?

Mr. CLAPPER. If you—do you mean the homeland or elsewhere in the world?

Senator GILLIBRAND. Your choice, but both would be good.

Mr. CLAPPER. Well, I think what they've tried—they're trying to do, of course, is to create the—both the substance and, maybe more importantly, the image of this global-scale caliphate by establishing chapters or franchises, if you will, in places like Libya, Egypt, Yemen, and South Asia. The extent to which, though, they—this is some monolithic organization, where ISIL in al-Rikah or Abu Du'a or Baghdadi is calling the shots in, say, Afghanistan/Pakistan, I don't see a lot of evidence of this. I think this is more about pledging allegiance to the brutality and the savagery of the—of ISIL. But, the first and foremost issues for these local chapters is local.

I think, aspirationally, there is a threat that ISIL poses, potentially, to the homeland, and those they might harbor in their area, particularly in Iraq and Syria, who would do us harm.

Senator GILLIBRAND. I agree with that assessment. And we just had a recent case out of Brooklyn, where we had threats being made.

You mentioned Yemen. Could you just briefly——

Mr. CLAPPER. If I——

Senator GILLIBRAND. Go ahead.

Mr. CLAPPER. If I might comment on that, ma'am, this is what I was referring to in my oral statement about—and this is a real challenge for all of us in—whether homeland security or intelligence—is the appeal, the rhetorical or spiritual appeal that, because of the effective—very highly effective media capabilities that ISIL has demonstrated, and how that—they are able to appeal to people, who then can act on their own at a time—in a time and place and circumstance of their choosing. And that is a very worrisome challenge, particularly in this country. So, not so much them commanding/controlling plots as much as——

Senator GILLIBRAND. Inspiring——

Mr. CLAPPER.—inspiring them.

Senator GILLIBRAND.—plots, right.

So, do you have recommendations for us about ways to stem that tide? Do you believe that our allies and other countries are doing their fair share? Particularly, I am concerned about the flow of foreign fighters, some of them from the United States, from Europe into—in and out of Syria. For example, what should Turkey be doing to help us more?

Mr. CLAPPER. Well, as we discussed before, Turkey has its own focus, which doesn't necessarily comport with ours, in terms of focusing on ISIL or al-Qaeda. They have very permissive laws. It would be good if they could—if we could—if they would change them to have more stringent controls over who transits through their country.

I do—I would volunteer that I think, because of the effectiveness of the media campaign or the propaganda campaign that ISIL mounts, that we, the United States, and we, the West, we who oppose ISIL need to be, I think, much more aggressive in mounting the counternarrative.

Senator GILLIBRAND. Thank you, Mr. Chairman.

Chairman MCCAIN. I want to thank the witnesses.

Just before we conclude, could I just, again, take a look at that chart over there—General, I know you've seen it—as to the expansion of the Chinese by filling in areas in the South China Sea.

That's a rather dramatic change, it seems to me. And obviously, they'd be filling in—that in, in order to place installations there. Is—could you talk a little bit about that before we conclude?

Mr. CLAPPER. Well, the Chinese, of course, have had their exorbitant claims, the so-called ''Nine-Dash line,'' throughout the South China Sea, been very aggressive about pursuing that. The—and, of course, this runs afoul of counterclaims that many of the other countries also have in the same area. And they, too, are very concerned about it. In fact, I think, in a sense, that's—that may be a good thing, because, in the end, their strength is going to be as—if an act—they can act collectively.

So, what the Chinese are doing, here, of course—in one case, you know, building airfield—an airdrome so that they can launch aircraft in and out to do patrols and surveillance and further exert what they consider is their sovereignty over the South China Sea. And it has been impressive, in the last year, year and a half since they've been doing this, as they pursued drilling, which has caused conflict with the Vietnamese and others. And so, this is a worrisome trend of the Chinese because of the tensions it's going to create in the South China Sea.

Chairman McCAIN. So, you've——

Mr. CLAPPER. But, they've been very aggressive about it.

Chairman McCAIN. So, you've got, not only the capability to build an airfield, but, obviously, weapon systems. Could also be—

Mr. CLAPPER. Well, they could, exactly.

Chairman McCAIN. Yeah.

Mr. CLAPPER. Of course, they're still in the construction phase, so what they actually deploy to something like this, or whether they permanently—they make it big enough so they could permanently station forces, that'll be interesting to see what they do.

Chairman McCAIN. Well, obviously our attention is on other parts of the world, but this is really quite a major step on their part. And I thank you for helping us out on that.

Jack, do you——

Senator REED. I'd—if I may, with just one question, in reaction to Senator Gillibrand's questioning.

We all understand, there's a huge, sort of, public campaign that ISIL is undertaking to attract recruits, to dramatize what they're doing. And you may not be able to comment in this setting. But, are we taking steps to interdict that communication so that they're not able to put things up and attract recruits and communicate?

Mr. CLAPPER. Well, the problem there is, their ubiquitous use of the media. And so, the challenge is, How do you take down the Internet? Because that's more and more what they're doing. In the day when al Qaeda or ISIL put these things out, it was kind of channelized, and we kind of watched it, and could do that. They've gotten wise to that, and now they make it very difficult, because of the universal forums and the way they get things out so ubiquitously. Very hard to control it. Ergo, what we must do, I believe, is counter the messages.

Senator REED. Thank you.

Thank you, Mr. Chairman.

Chairman McCAIN. General, I know you've had a—are going to have and are having a very busy couple of days, and I know you understand that we have our responsibilities to try to inform members in the Senate so that we can shape legislation to help you do your job more effectively and efficiently.

And we thank both of you for being here.

This hearing is adjourned.

[Whereupon, at 11:28 a.m., the committee adjourned.]